C000065261

Teacher's Guide 1

Composition Skills

Author: Chris Whitney

William Collins' dream of knowledge for all began with the publication of his first book in 1819.

A self-educated mill worker, he not only enriched millions of lives, but also founded a flourishing publishing house. Today, staying true to this spirit, Collins books are packed with inspiration, innovation and practical expertise. They place you at the centre of a world of possibility and give you exactly what you need to explore it.

Collins. Freedom to teach.

Published by Collins
An imprint of HarperCollins*Publishers*
The News Building
1 London Bridge Street
London
SE1 9GF

Browse the complete Collins catalogue at
www.collins.co.uk

© HarperCollins*Publishers* Limited 2017

10 9 8 7 6 5 4 3 2 1

ISBN 978-0-00-822302-1

British Library Cataloguing in Publication Data

A catalogue record for this publication is available from the British Library.

Publishing Director: Lee Newman
Publishing Manager: Helen Doran
Senior Editor: Hannah Dove
Project Manager: Emily Hooton
Author: Chris Whitney
Development Editors: Robert Anderson and Sarah Snashall
Copy-editor: Trish Chapman
Proofreader: Tracy Thomas
Cover design and artwork: Amparo Barrera and Ken Vail Graphic Design
Internal design concept: Amparo Barrera
Typesetter: Ken Vail Graphic Design
Illustrations: Alberto Saichann (Beehive Illustration)
Production Controller: Rachel Weaver

Printed and bound by
CPI Group (UK) Ltd, Croydon, CR0 4YY

Acknowledgements

The publishers wish to thank the following for permission to reproduce content. Every effort has been made to trace copyright holders and to obtain their permission for the use of copyright materials. The publishers will gladly receive any information enabling them to rectify any error or omission at the first opportunity.

HarperCollins Publishers Ltd for an extract on page 56 from *Meg, Mum and the Donkey* by Simon Puttock, copyright © 2013 Simon Puttock, 2005; and for an extract on page 62 from *Time for school* by Wendy Cope, copyright © 2013 Wendy Cope. Reproduced by permission of HarperCollins Publishers Ltd.

Contents

About Treasure House 4

Support, embed and challenge 12

Assessment 13

Support with teaching composition 14

Delivering the 2014 National Curriculum for English 15

Unit 1: Stories in familiar settings (1) 23

Unit 2: Fairy stories 25

Unit 3: Fantasy stories (1) 27

Unit 4: Poetry: The senses 29

Unit 5: Poetry: Patterns 31

Unit 6: Poetry: My favourite 33

Unit 7: Writing instructions (1) 35

Review unit 1 37

Unit 8: Writing simple reports (1) 38

Unit 9: Writing simple recounts 40

Unit 10: Traditional tales 42

Unit 11: Writing simple reports (2) 44

Unit 12: Stories in familiar settings (2) 46

Unit 13: Fables (1) 48

Unit 14: Writing instructions (2) 50

Review unit 2 52

Unit 15: Writing simple reports (3) 53

Unit 16: Fables (2) 55

Unit 17: Stories in familiar settings (3) 57

Unit 18: Writing simple reports (4) 59

Unit 19: Information writing 61

Unit 20: Fantasy stories (2) 63

Review unit 3 65

Photocopiable resources 66

About Treasure House

Treasure House is a comprehensive and flexible bank of books and online resources for teaching the English curriculum. The Treasure House series offers two different pathways: one covering each English strand discretely (Skills Focus Pathway) and one integrating texts and the strands to create a programme of study (Integrated English Pathway). This Teacher's Guide is part of the Skills Focus Pathway.

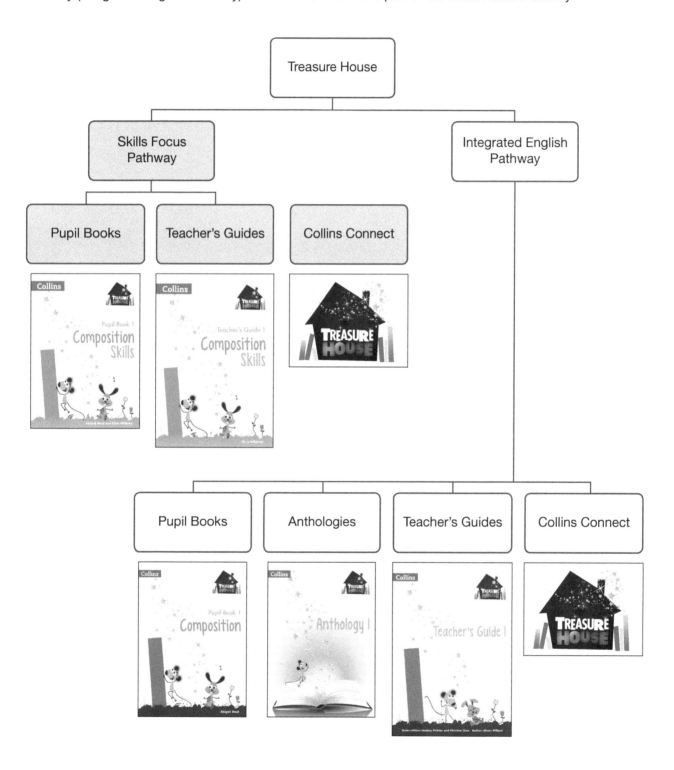

1. Skills Focus

The Skills Focus Pupil Books and Teacher's Guides for all four strands (Comprehension; Spelling; Composition; and Vocabulary, Grammar and Punctuation) allow you to teach each curriculum area in a targeted way. Each unit in the Pupil Book is mapped directly to the statutory requirements of the National Curriculum. Each Teacher's Guide provides step-by-step instructions to guide you through the Pupil Book activities and digital Collins Connect resources for each competency. With a clear focus on skills and clearly-listed curriculum objectives you can select the appropriate resources to support your lessons.

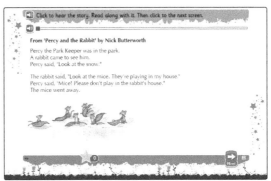

2. Integrated English

Alternatively, the Integrated English pathway offers a complete programme of genre-based teaching sequences. There is one Teacher's Guide and one Anthology for each year group. Each Teacher's Guide provides 15 teaching sequences focused on different genres of text such as fairy tales, letters and newspaper articles. The Anthologies contain the classic texts, fiction, non-fiction and poetry required for each sequence. Each sequence also weaves together all four dimensions of the National Curriculum for English – Comprehension; Spelling; Composition; and Vocabulary, Grammar and Punctuation – into a complete English programme. The Pupil Books and Collins Connect provide targeted explanation of key points and practice activities organised by strand. This programme provides 30 weeks of teaching inspiration.

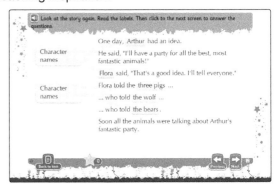

Other components

Handwriting Books, Handwriting Workbooks, Word Books and the online digital resources on Collins Connect are suitable for use with both pathways.

Treasure House Skills Focus Teacher's Guides

Year	Comprehension	Composition	Vocabulary, Grammar and Punctuation	Spelling
1	978-0-00-822290-1	978-0-00-822302-1	978-0-00-822296-3	978-0-00-822308-3
2	978-0-00-822291-8	978-0-00-822303-8	978-0-00-822297-0	978-0-00-822309-0
3	978-0-00-822292-5	978-0-00-822304-5	978-0-00-822298-7	978-0-00-822310-6
4	978-0-00-822293-2	978-0-00-822305-2	978-0-00-822299-4	978-0-00-822311-3
5	978-0-00-822294-9	978-0-00-822306-9	978-0-00-822300-7	978-0-00-822312-0
6	978-0-00-822295-6	978-0-00-822307-6	978-0-00-822301-4	978-0-00-822313-7

Inside the Skills Focus Teacher's Guides

The teaching notes in each unit in the Teacher's Guide provide you with subject information or background, a range of whole class and differentiated activities including photocopiable resource sheets and links to the Pupil Book and the online Collins Connect activities.

Each **Overview** provides clear objectives for each lesson tied into the new curriculum, links to the other relevant components and a list of any additional resources required.

Teaching overview provides a brief introduction to the specific skill concept or text type and some pointers on how to approach it.

Support, embed & challenge supports a mastery approach with activities provided at three levels.

Unit 2: Fairy stories

Overview

English curriculum objectives

Reading: Year 1 pupils should be very familiar with key stories, fairy stories and traditional tales, retelling them and considering their particular characteristics.

Writing: Year 1 pupils should be taught to write sentences by:
- saying out loud what they are going to write about
- composing a sentence orally before writing it
- sequencing sentences to form short narratives
- beginning to punctuate sentences using a capital letter and a full stop.

Building towards

Children will explore, discuss and write about a fairy story.

Treasure House resources
- Composition Skills Pupil Book 1, Unit 2, pages 6–7
- Collins Connect Treasure House Composition Year 1 Unit 2
- Photocopiable Unit 2, Resource 1: My pictures for Rumpelstiltskin, page 68
- Photocopiable Unit 2, Resource 2: Speech bubbles for Rumpelstiltskin, page 69

Additional resources
- A modern retelling of the fairy story Rumpelstiltskin

Introduction

Teaching overview

This unit focuses on the fairy story Rumpelstiltskin. This is one of the many tales included by the German philologists Jakob (1785–1863) and Wilhelm (1786–59) Grimm in their 1812 collection of fairy tales *Children's and Household Tales*, though elements of the tale can be found in far older stories from around the world. Children read a short extract and consider the characters. It provides an opportunity to consider character in fairy stories and to orally rehearse prior to writing.

Introduce the concept

Ask the children what fairy stories they know. Take feedback and ask if they know the story of Rumpelstiltskin. Provide a summary. It would be helpful to have a copy of the full fairy tale to read to the class at some point, perhaps at the close of the session.

Pupil practice   Pupil Book pages 6–7

Get started

Children read the story and add the missing words to the text.

Answers

1. upon	[1 mark]
2. foolish	[1 mark]
3. daughter	[1 mark]
4. wanted	[1 mark]
5. king's	[1 mark]

Try these

Children add their own words to the sentences. Accept appropriate answers.

Possible answers

1. poor/silly
2. greedy
3. normal/ordinary
4. big/grand
5. yellow/dry   [1 mark per acceptable answer]

Now try these

Children draw pictures of the miller and the king at their respective homes. They add speech bubbles showing what each character might be saying. This should be rehearsed beforehand, possibly through role-play or hot-seating. Finally, they write a sentence about the miller telling a lie to the king.

25   26

Unit 2: Fairy stories

Support, embed & challenge

Support

Children use Unit 2 Resource 1: My pictures for Rumpelstiltskin to draw the characters and their homes and label each one correctly.

Embed

Children add speech into the speech bubbles provided in Unit 2 Resource 2: Speech bubbles for Rumpelstiltskin.

Challenge

Children read the full story and write sentences to retell it, starting after the extract.

Homework / Additional activities

Traditional tales to share

Ask the children to find and read other fairy stories or traditional tales at home. They could bring one into school to share with the class or, if they know the story, they could tell it to the class.

Collins Connect: Unit 2

Ask the children to complete Unit 2 (see Teach → Year 1 → Composition → Unit 2).

Pupil practice gives guidance and the answers to each of the three sections in the Pupil Book: *Get started*, *Try these* and *Now try these*.

Introduce the concept/text provides 5–10 minutes of preliminary discussion points or class/group activities to get the pupils engaged in the lesson focus and set out any essential prior learning.

Homework / Additional activities lists ideas for classroom or homework activities, and relevant activities from Collins Connect.

Two photocopiable resource worksheets per unit provide differentiated support for the writing task in each lesson. They are designed to be used with the activities in support or embed sections.

Treasure House Skills Focus Pupil Books

There are four Skills Focus Pupil Books for each year group, based on the four dimensions of the National Curriculum for English: Comprehension; Spelling; Composition; and Vocabulary, Grammar and Punctuation. The Pupil Books provide a child-friendly introduction to each subject and a range of initial activities for independent pupil-led learning. A Review unit for each term assesses pupils' progress.

Year	Comprehension	Composition	Vocabulary, Grammar and Punctuation	Spelling
1	978-0-00-823634-2	978-0-00-823646-5	978-0-00-823640-3	978-0-00-823652-6
2	978-0-00-823635-9	978-0-00-823647-2	978-0-00-823641-0	978-0-00-823653-3
3	978-0-00-823636-6	978-0-00-823648-9	978-0-00-823642-7	978-0-00-823654-0
4	978-0-00-823637-3	978-0-00-823649-6	978-0-00-823643-4	978-0-00-823655-7
5	978-0-00-823638-0	978-0-00-823650-2	978-0-00-823644-1	978-0-00-823656-4
6	978-0-00-823639-7	978-0-00-823651-9	978-0-00-823645-8	978-0-00-823657-1

Inside the Skills Focus Pupil Books

Comprehension

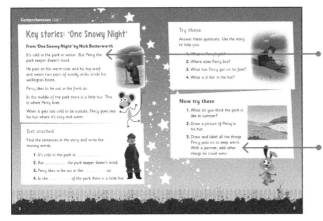

Includes high-quality text extracts covering poetry, prose, traditional tales, playscripts and non-fiction.

Pupils retrieve and record information, learn to draw inferences from texts and increase their familiarity with a wide range of literary genres.

Composition

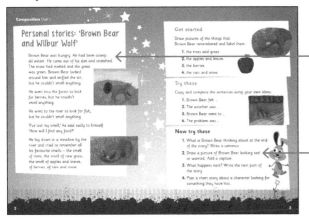

Includes high-quality, annotated text extracts as models for different types of writing.

Children learn how to write effectively and for a purpose.

Vocabulary, Grammar and Punctuation

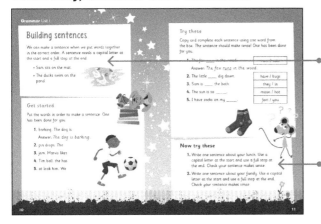

Develops children's knowledge and understanding of grammar and punctuation skills.

A rule is introduced and explained. Children are given lots of opportunities to practise using it.

Spelling

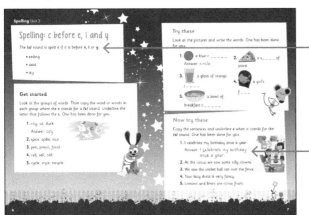

Spelling rules are introduced and explained.

Practice is provided for spotting and using the spelling rules, correcting misspelt words and using the words in context.

Treasure House on Collins Connect

Digital resources for Treasure House are available on Collins Connect which provides a wealth of interactive activities. Treasure House is organised into six core areas on Collins Connect:

- Comprehension
- Spelling
- Composition
- Vocabulary, Grammar and Punctuation
- The Reading Attic
- Teacher's Guides and Anthologies.

For most units in the Skills Focus Pupil Books, there is an accompanying Collins Connect unit focused on the same teaching objective. These fun, independent activities can be used for initial pupil-led learning, or for further practice using a different learning environment. Either way, with Collins Connect, you have a wealth of questions to help children embed their learning.

Treasure House on Collins Connect is available via subscription at connect.collins.co.uk

Features of Treasure House on Collins Connect

The digital resources enhance children's comprehension, spelling, composition, and vocabulary, grammar, punctuation skills through providing:

- a bank of varied and engaging interactive activities so children can practise their skills independently
- audio support to help children access the texts and activities
- auto-mark functionality so children receive instant feedback and have the opportunity to repeat tasks.

Teachers benefit from useful resources and time-saving tools including:

- teacher-facing materials such as audio and explanations for front-of-class teaching or pupil-led learning
- lesson starter videos for some Composition units
- downloadable teaching notes for all online activities
- downloadable teaching notes for Skills Focus and Integrated English pathways
- the option to assign homework activities to your classes
- class records to monitor progress.

Comprehension

- Includes high-quality text extracts covering poetry, prose, traditional tales, playscripts and non-fiction.
- Audio function supports children to access the text and the activities

Composition

- Activities support children to develop and build more sophisticated sentence structures.
- Every unit ends with a longer piece of writing that can be submitted to the teacher for marking.

Vocabulary, Grammar and Punctuation

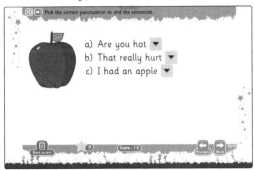

- Fun, practical activities develop children's knowledge and understanding of grammar and punctuation skills.
- Each skill is reinforced with a huge, varied bank of practice questions.

Spelling

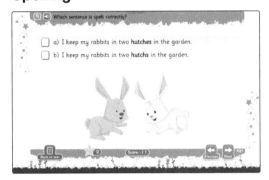

- Fun, practical activities develop children's knowledge and understanding of each spelling rule.
- Each rule is reinforced with a huge, varied bank of practice questions.
- Children spell words using an audio prompt, write their own sentences and practise spelling using Look Say Cover Write Check.

Reading Attic

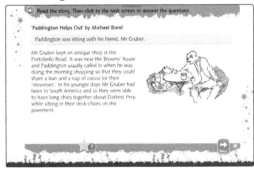

- Children's love of reading is nurtured with texts from exciting children's authors including Michael Bond, David Walliams and Michael Morpurgo.
- Lesson sequences accompany the texts, with drama opportunities and creative strategies for engaging children with key themes, characters and plots.
- Whole-book projects encourage reading for pleasure.

Treasure House Digital Teacher's Guides and Anthologies

The teaching sequences and anthology texts for each year group are included as a flexible bank of resources.

The teaching notes for each skill strand and year group are also included on Collins Connect.

Support, embed and challenge

Treasure House provides comprehensive, detailed differentiation at three levels to ensure that all children are able to access achievement. It is important that children master the basic skills before they go further in their learning. Children may make progress towards the standard at different speeds, with some not reaching it until the very end of the year.

In the Teacher's Guide, Support, Embed and Challenge sections allow teachers to keep the whole class focussed with no child left behind. Two photocopiable resources per unit offer additional material linked to the Support, Embed or Challenge sections.

Support

The Support section offers simpler or more scaffolded activities that will help learners who have not yet grasped specific concepts covered. Background information may also be provided to help children to contextualise learning. This enables children to make progress so that they can keep up with the class.

To help with children's composition skills, activities are broken down into smaller steps, for example, children draw pictures, write plans or complete templates before writing sentences.

If you have a teaching assistant, you may wish to ask him or her to help children work through these activities. You might then ask children who have completed these activities to progress to other more challenging tasks found in the Embed or Challenge sections – or you may decide more practice of the basics is required. Collins Connect can provide further activities.

Embed

The Embed section includes activities to embed learning and is aimed at those who children who are working at the expected standard. It ensures that learners have understood key teaching objectives for the age-group. These activities could be used by the whole class or groups, and most are appropriate for both teacher-led and independent work.

In Composition, children can practise their writing skills using templates, plans and prompts allowing them to write a variety of text-types at the required standard.

Challenge

The Challenge section provides additional tasks, questions or activities that will push children who have mastered the concept without difficulty. This keeps children motivated and allows them to gain a greater depth of understanding. You may wish to give these activities to fast finishers to work through independently.

In Composition, children's writing skills can be enhanced with the freer activities in the Challenge section, for example, they may write an alternative ending to a story, retell a story in their own words or think about a story from another perspective. Children can demonstrate more advanced use of vocabulary and manipulate grammar more accurately through these tasks.

Assessment

Teacher's Guide

There are opportunities for assessment throughout the Treasure House series. The teaching notes in Treasure House Teacher's Guides offer ideas for questions, informal assessment and spelling tests.

Pupil Book Review units

Each Pupil Book has three Review units designed as a quick formative assessment tool for the end of each term. Questions assess the work that has been covered over the previous units. These review units will provide you with an informal way of measuring your pupils' progress. You may wish to use these as Assessment for Learning to help you and your pupils to understand where they are in their learning journey.

In Treasure House, there is a strong focus on genres of texts that widen children's knowledge of writing for different purposes and audiences. In Composition, the review units allow children to demonstrate what they know in independent tasks. Vocabulary, grammar and punctuation can be assessed through their writing as well as their understanding of a genre.

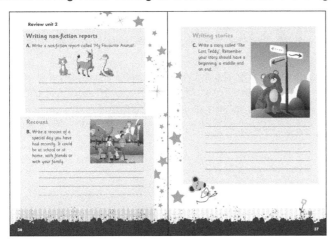

Assessment in Collins Connect

Activities on Collins Connect can also be used for effective assessment. Activities with auto-marking mean that if children answer incorrectly, they can make another attempt helping them to analyse their own work for mistakes. Homework activities can also be assigned to classes through Collins Connect. At the end of activities, children can select a smiley face to indicate how they found the task giving you useful feedback on any gaps in knowledge.

Class records on Collins Connect allow you to get an overview of children's progress with several features. You can choose to view records by unit, pupil or strand. By viewing detailed scores, you can view pupils' scores question by question in a clear table-format to help you establish areas where there might be particular strengths and weaknesses both class-wide and for individuals.

If you wish, you can also set mastery judgements (mastery achieved and exceeded, mastery achieved, mastery not yet achieved) to help see where your children need more help.

Support with teaching composition

Composition is one of the four core dimensions of the National Curriculum for English. Within the teaching of English, the aim is to ensure that all pupils write clearly, accurately and coherently, adapting their language and style in and for a range of contexts, purposes and audiences.

Effective composition involves forming, articulating and communicating ideas, and then organising them coherently for a reader. This requires clarity and an awareness of the audience, purpose and context. All children can be helped towards better writing if shown how to generate and organise ideas appropriately and how to then transfer them successfully from plan to page. In addition, pupils need to be taught how to plan, revise and evaluate their writing. These aspects of writing have been incorporated into the Treasure House Composition Skills strand.

Throughout the primary years, we want pupils to have opportunities to write for a range of real purposes and audiences as part of their work across the curriculum. These purposes and audiences should underpin the decisions about the form the writing should take, such as a narrative, an explanation or a description. We want pupils to develop positive attitudes towards their writing and stamina for it by writing narratives about personal experiences and those of others, by writing about real events, by writing poetry and by writing for different purposes.

Pupils also need to be taught to monitor whether their own writing makes sense. They should also understand, through being shown, the skills and processes essential for writing: the generation of ideas, initial drafting, and re-reading to check that the meaning is clear.

Treasure House Composition Skills Teacher's Guides provide extensive notes and guidance for teaching a range of genres and text types. The integrated pupil books provide opportunities for pupils to plan, draft and edit their writing. Each unit is linked to an extract of quality text from which the teaching ideas are taken.

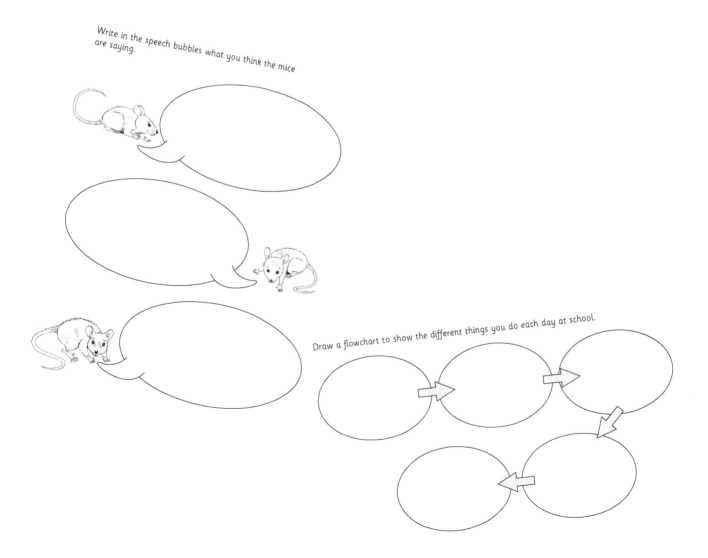

Delivering the 2014 National Curriculum for English

Unit	Title	Treasure House Resources	Collins Connect	English Programme of Study
1	Stories with familiar settings (1)	• Composition Skills Pupil Book 1, Unit 1, pages 4–5 • Composition Skills Teacher's Guide 1 – Unit 1, pages 23–24 – Photocopiable Unit 1, Resource 1: My picture of the park, page 66 – Photocopiable Unit 1, Resource 2: Mouse speech bubbles, page 67	Collins Connect Treasure House Composition Year 1, Unit 1	**Reading:** Becoming very familiar with key stories, fairy stories and traditional tales, retelling them and considering their particular characteristics. **Writing:** Saying out loud what they are going to write about. Composing a sentence orally before writing it. Sequencing sentences to form short narratives. Beginning to punctuate sentences using a capital letter and a full stop.
2	Fairy stories	• Composition Skills Pupil Book 1, Unit 2, pages 6–7 • Composition Skills Teacher's Guide 1 – Unit 2, pages 25–26 – Photocopiable Unit 2, Resource 1: My pictures for Rumpelstiltskin, page 68 – Photocopiable Unit 2, Resource 2: Speech bubbles for Rumpelstiltskin, page 69	Collins Connect Treasure House Composition Year 1, Unit 2	**Reading:** Becoming very familiar with key stories, fairy stories and traditional tales, retelling them and considering their particular characteristics. **Writing:** Saying out loud what they are going to write about. Composing a sentence orally before writing it. Sequencing sentences to form short narratives. Beginning to punctuate sentences using a capital letter and a full stop.
3	Fantasy stories (1)	• Composition Skills Pupil Book 1, Unit 3, pages 8–9 • Composition Skills Teacher's Guide 1 – Unit 3, pages 27–28 – Photocopiable Unit 3, Resource 1: My fantastic party animal, page 70 – Photocopiable Unit 3, Resource 2: Arthur's party invitation, page 71	Collins Connect Treasure House Composition Year 1, Unit 3	**Reading:** Becoming very familiar with key stories, fairy stories and traditional tales, retelling them and considering their particular characteristics. **Writing:** Saying out loud what they are going to write about. Composing a sentence orally before writing it. Sequencing sentences to form short narratives. Beginning to punctuate sentences using a capital letter and a full stop.

Unit	Title	Treasure House Resources	Collins Connect	English Programme of Study

4	Poetry: The senses	• Composition Skills Pupil Book 1, Unit 4, pages 10–11
		• Composition Skills Teacher's Guide 1
		  – Unit 4, pages 29–30
		  – Photocopiable Unit 4, Resource 1: Night-time sounds, page 72
		  – Photocopiable Unit 4, Resource 2: What I hear at night, page 73
			Collins Connect Treasure House Composition Year 1, Unit 4	**Reading:** Developing pleasure in reading, motivation to read, vocabulary and understanding by listening to and discussing a wide range of poems, stories and non-fiction at a level beyond that at which they can read independently.
				Writing: Saying out loud what they are going to write about.
				Composing a sentence orally before writing it.
				Sequencing sentences to form short narratives.
				Beginning to punctuate sentences using a capital letter and a full stop.

5	Poetry: Patterns	• Composition Skills Pupil Book 1, Unit 5, pages 12–13
		• Composition Skills Teacher's Guide 1
		  – Unit 5, pages 31–32
		  – Photocopiable Unit 5, Resource 1: Mum and boy's speech bubbles, page 74
		  – Photocopiable Unit 5, Resource 2: I still love you! page 75
			Collins Connect Treasure House Composition Year 1, Unit 5	**Reading:** Developing pleasure in reading, motivation to read, vocabulary and understanding by listening to and discussing a wide range of poems, stories and non-fiction at a level beyond that at which they can read independently.
				Writing: Saying out loud what they are going to write about.
				Composing a sentence orally before writing it.
				Sequencing sentences to form short narratives.
				Beginning to punctuate sentences using a capital letter and a full stop.

6	Poetry: My favourite	• Composition Skills Pupil Book 1, Unit 6, pages 14–15
		• Composition Skills Teacher's Guide 1
		  – Unit 6, pages 33–34
		  – Photocopiable Unit 6, Resource 1: My underwater picture, page 76
		  – Photocopiable Unit 6, Resource 2: All at sea, page 77
		  – Photocopiable Unit 6, Resource 3: Sea creature, page 78
			Collins Connect Treasure House Composition Year 1, Unit 6	**Reading:** Developing pleasure in reading, motivation to read, vocabulary and understanding by listening to and discussing a wide range of poems, stories and non-fiction at a level beyond that at which they can read independently.
				Writing: Saying out loud what they are going to write about.
				Composing a sentence orally before writing it.
				Sequencing sentences to form short narratives.
				Beginning to punctuate sentences using a capital letter and a full stop.

Unit	Title	Treasure House Resources	Collins Connect	English Programme of Study

7	Writing instructions (1)	• Composition Skills Pupil Book 1, Unit 7, pages 16–17
		• Composition Skills Teacher's Guide 1
		  – Unit 7, pages 35–36
		  – Photocopiable Unit 7, Resource 1: My instructions for growing a beanstalk, page 79
		  – Photocopiable Unit 7, Resource 2: Welcome to our class, page 80
			Collins Connect Treasure House Composition Year 1, Unit 7	**Reading:** Developing pleasure in reading, motivation to read, vocabulary and understanding by listening to and discussing a wide range of poems, stories and non-fiction at a level beyond that at which they can read independently.
				Writing: Saying out loud what they are going to write about.
				Composing a sentence orally before writing it.
				Sequencing sentences to form short narratives.
				Beginning to punctuate sentences using a capital letter and a full stop.

8	Writing simple reports (1)	• Composition Skills Pupil Book 1, Unit 8, pages 20–21
		• Composition Skills Teacher's Guide 1
		  – Unit 8, pages 38–39
		  – Photocopiable Unit 8, Resource 1: My picture of a robin, page 81
		  – Photocopiable Unit 8, Resource 2: My report on a bird, page 82
			Collins Connect Treasure House Composition Year 1, Unit 8	**Reading:** Developing pleasure in reading, motivation to read, vocabulary and understanding by listening to and discussing a wide range of poems, stories and non-fiction at a level beyond that at which they can read independently.
				Writing: Saying out loud what they are going to write about.
				Composing a sentence orally before writing it.
				Sequencing sentences.
				Beginning to punctuate sentences using a capital letter and a full stop.

9	Writing simple recounts	• Composition Skills Pupil Book 1, Unit 9, pages 22–23
		• Composition Skills Teacher's Guide 1
		  – Unit 9, pages 40–41
		  – Photocopiable Unit 9, Resource 1: What I did on my birthday, page 83
		  – Photocopiable Unit 9, Resource 2: What my friend did yesterday, page 84
			Collins Connect Treasure House Composition Year 1, Unit 9	**Reading:** Developing pleasure in reading, motivation to read, vocabulary and understanding by listening to and discussing a wide range of poems, stories and non-fiction at a level beyond that at which they can read independently.
				Writing: Saying out loud what they are going to write about.
				Composing a sentence orally before writing it.
				Sequencing sentences.
				Beginning to punctuate sentences using a capital letter and a full stop.

Unit	Title	Treasure House Resources	Collins Connect	English Programme of Study

10	Traditional tales	• Composition Skills Pupil Book 1, Unit 10, pages 24–26
		• Composition Skills Teacher's Guide 1
		  – Unit 10, pages 42–43
		  – Photocopiable Unit 10, Resource 1: My picture of what happens next, page 85
		  – Photocopiable Unit 10, Resource 2: Once upon a time, page 86
				Reading: Becoming very familiar with key stories, fairy stories and traditional tales, retelling them and considering their particular characteristics.
				Writing: Saying out loud what they are going to write about.
				Composing a sentence orally before writing it.
				Sequencing sentences to form short narratives.
				Beginning to punctuate sentences using a capital letter and a full stop, question mark or exclamation mark.

11	Writing simple reports (2)	• Composition Skills Pupil Book 1, Unit 11, pages 27–28
		• Composition Skills Teacher's Guide 1
		  – Unit 11, pages 44–45
		  – Photocopiable Unit 11, Resource 1: Fantastic zebras and giraffes, page 87
		  – Photocopiable Unit 11, Resource 2: My animal report, page 88
				Reading: Developing pleasure in reading, motivation to read, vocabulary and understanding by listening to and discussing a wide range of poems, stories and non-fiction at a level beyond that at which they can read independently.
				Writing: Saying out loud what they are going to write about.
				Composing a sentence orally before writing it.
				Sequencing sentences.
				Beginning to punctuate sentences using a capital letter and a full stop.

12	Stories in familiar settings (2)	• Composition Skills Pupil Book 1, Unit 12, pages 29–31
		• Composition Skills Teacher's Guide 1
		  – Unit 12, pages 46–47
		  – Photocopiable Unit 12, Resource 1: How naughty! page 89
		  – Photocopiable Unit 12, Resource 2: What a naughty animal, page 90
				Reading: Becoming very familiar with key stories, fairy stories and traditional tales, retelling them and considering their particular characteristics.
				Writing: Saying out loud what they are going to write about.
				Composing a sentence orally before writing it.
				Sequencing sentences to form short narratives.
				Beginning to punctuate sentences using a capital letter and a full stop, question mark or exclamation mark.

Unit	Title	Treasure House Resources	Collins Connect	English Programme of Study

13	Fables (1)	• Composition Skills Pupil Book 1, Unit 13, pages 32–33
		• Composition Skills Teacher's Guide 1
		  – Unit 13, pages 48–49
		  – Photocopiable Unit 13, Resource 1: My ending, page 91
		  – Photocopiable Unit 13, Resource 2: The Lion and the Mouse, page 92
				Reading: Becoming very familiar with key stories, fairy stories and traditional tales, retelling them and considering their particular characteristics.
				Writing: Saying out loud what they are going to write about.
				Composing a sentence orally before writing it.
				Sequencing sentences to form short narratives.
				Beginning to punctuate sentences using a capital letter and a full stop, question mark or exclamation mark.

14	Writing instructions (2)	• Composition Skills Pupil Book 1, Unit 14, pages 34–35
		• Composition Skills Teacher's Guide 1
		  – Unit 14, pages 50–51
		  – Photocopiable Unit 14, Resource 1: My flowchart for keeping a worm, page 93
		  – Photocopiable Unit 14, Resource 2: How to keep a worm, page 94
				Reading: Developing pleasure in reading, motivation to read, vocabulary and understanding by listening to and discussing a wide range of poems, stories and non-fiction at a level beyond that at which they can read independently.
				Writing: Saying out loud what they are going to write about.
				Composing a sentence orally before writing it.
				Sequencing sentences.
				Beginning to punctuate sentences using a capital letter and a full stop, question mark or exclamation mark.

Unit	Title	Treasure House Resources	Collins Connect	English Programme of Study

15	Writing simple reports (3)	• Composition Skills Pupil Book 1, Unit 15, pages 38–40
		• Composition Skills Teacher's Guide 1
		  – Unit 15, pages 53–54
		  – Photocopiable Unit 15, Resource 1: My polar bear report, page 95
		  – Photocopiable Unit 15, Resource 2: Polar bear fact file, page 96
				Reading: Developing pleasure in reading, motivation to read, vocabulary and understanding by listening to and discussing a wide range of poems, stories and non-fiction at a level beyond that at which they can read independently.
				Writing: Saying out loud what they are going to write about.
				Composing a sentence orally before writing it.
				Sequencing sentences.
				Beginning to punctuate sentences using a capital letter and a full stop, question mark or exclamation mark.

16	Fables (2)	• Composition Skills Pupil Book 1, Unit 16, pages 41–42
		• Composition Skills Teacher's Guide 1
		  – Unit 16, pages 55–56
		  – Photocopiable Unit 16, Resource 1: My ending for the fable, page 97
		  – Photocopiable Unit 16, Resource 2: My recount of the fable, page 98
				Reading: Becoming very familiar with key stories, fairy stories and traditional tales, retelling them and considering their particular characteristics.
				Writing: Saying out loud what they are going to write about.
				Composing a sentence orally before writing it.
				Sequencing sentences to form short narratives.
				Beginning to punctuate sentences using a capital letter and a full stop, question mark or exclamation mark.

17	Stories in familiar settings (3)	• Composition Skills Pupil Book 1, Unit 17, pages 43–44
		• Composition Skills Teacher's Guide 1
		  – Unit 17, pages 57–58
		  – Photocopiable Unit 17, Resource 1: The frog's day, page 99
		  – Photocopiable Unit 17, Resource 2: My recount of 'Doing Nothing!' page 100
				Reading: Becoming very familiar with key stories, fairy stories and traditional tales, retelling them and considering their particular characteristics.
				Writing: Saying out loud what they are going to write about.
				Composing a sentence orally before writing it.
				Sequencing sentences to form short narratives.
				Beginning to punctuate sentences using a capital letter and a full stop, question mark or exclamation mark.

Unit	Title	Treasure House Resources	Collins Connect	English Programme of Study
18	Writing simple reports (4)	• Composition Skills Pupil Book 1, Unit 18, pages 45–46 • Composition Skills Teacher's Guide 1 – Unit 18, pages 59–60 – Photocopiable Unit 18, Resource 1: My home, page 101 – Photocopiable Unit 18, Resource 2: Information report on my home, page 102		**Reading:** Developing pleasure in reading, motivation to read, vocabulary and understanding by listening to and discussing a wide range of poems, stories and non-fiction at a level beyond that at which they can read independently. **Writing:** Saying out loud what they are going to write about. Composing a sentence orally before writing it. Sequencing sentences. Beginning to punctuate sentences using a capital letter and a full stop, question mark or exclamation mark.
19	Information writing	• Composition Skills Pupil Book 1, Unit 19, pages 47–49 • Composition Skills Teacher's Guide 1 – Unit 19, pages 61–62 – Photocopiable Unit 19, Resource 1: My 'school day' flowchart, page 103 – Photocopiable Unit 19, Resource 2: My 'school day' storyboard, page 104		**Reading:** Developing pleasure in reading, motivation to read, vocabulary and understanding by listening to and discussing a wide range of poems, stories and non-fiction at a level beyond that at which they can read independently. **Writing:** Saying out loud what they are going to write about. Composing a sentence orally before writing it. Sequencing sentences to form short narratives. Beginning to punctuate sentences using a capital letter and a full stop, question mark or exclamation mark.

Unit	Title	Treasure House Resources	Collins Connect	English Programme of Study
20	Fantasy stories (2)	• Composition Skills Pupil Book 1, Unit 20, pages 50–53 • Composition Skills Teacher's Guide 1 – Unit 20, pages 63–64 – Photocopiable Unit 20, Resource 1: My rocket, page 105 – Photocopiable Unit 20, Resource 2: My rocket: plan and story, page 106–107		**Reading:** Developing pleasure in reading, motivation to read, vocabulary and understanding by listening to and discussing a wide range of poems, stories and non-fiction at a level beyond that at which they can read independently. **Writing:** Saying out loud what they are going to write about. Composing a sentence orally before writing it. Sequencing sentences to form short narratives. Beginning to punctuate sentences using a capital letter and a full stop, question mark or exclamation mark.
	All units	The following statutory requirements can be covered throughout the programme: Pupils should be taught to: • write sentences by: – re-reading what they have written to check that it makes sense • discuss what they have written with the teacher or other pupils • read aloud their writing clearly enough to be heard by their peers and the teacher.		

Unit 1: Stories in familiar settings (1)

Overview

English curriculum objectives

Reading: Year 1 pupils should be very familiar with key stories, fairy stories and traditional tales, retelling them and considering their particular characteristics.

Writing: Year 1 pupils should be taught to write sentences by:

- saying out loud what they are going to write about
- composing a sentence orally before writing it
- sequencing sentences to form short narratives
- beginning to punctuate sentences using a capital letter and a full stop.

Building towards

Children will explore, discuss and write about a story set in a park.

Treasure House resources

- Composition Skills Pupil Book 1, Unit 1, pages 4–5
- Collins Connect Treasure House Composition Year 1 Unit 1
- Photocopiable Unit 1, Resource 1: My picture of the park, page 66
- Photocopiable Unit 1, Resource 2: Mouse speech bubbles, page 67

Additional resources

- A variety of stories set in familiar settings for children to read
- *Percy and the Rabbit* and other books in the 'Percy the Park Keeper' series by Nick Butterworth
- Other stories about mice or where the setting is a park

Introduction

Teaching overview

This unit focuses on stories in familiar settings. It provides the children with the opportunity to become familiar with such texts, discussing setting and character. It also gives them the chance to rehearse their ideas and sentences orally prior to writing.

The unit uses as its base text an excerpt from *Percy and the Rabbit* (2005) by the British author and illustrator Nick Butterworth (born 1946).

Introduce the concept

Ask the children to share and talk about their trips to a park, describing what the park is like and whether they have ever seen a park keeper. Ask: 'What did he or she look like?' Discuss what kind of things the children think the park keeper does as part of his or her job.

Ask: 'Have you ever seen any animals in the park?' and then, specifically, 'Have you ever seen a mouse in the park?' Take feedback and show pictures of mice, if necessary.

Pupil practice

Pupil Book pages 4–5

Get started

Children read the extract and add the missing words to the text.

Answers

1. park	[1 mark]
2. rabbit	[1 mark]
3. snow	[1 mark]
4. mice	[1 mark]
5. house	[1 mark]

Try these

Children add their own words to the sentences. Accept appropriate answers.

Possible answers

1. upset
2. happy/helpful
3. playing/naughty
4. snowy/cold
5. warm/cosy   [1 mark per acceptable answer]

Now try these

Children draw a picture of the park and discuss with a partner what they think the rabbit's house looks like. They then draw the mice playing in the rabbit's house.

They discuss with a partner what they think the mice are saying and add this to speech bubbles in their pictures.

You may wish to use the activities and photocopiables in **Support and Embed** to give differentiated support with the tasks in **Now try these**

Support, embed & challenge

Support

Ask the children to focus on **Now try these** questions 1 and 2. Children use Unit 1 Resource 1: My picture of the park to draw a picture of the park and add the rabbit's house. Ask them to add labels to their picture. Ask them to show their picture to a partner and tell their partner what the mice are saying.

Embed

After the children have drawn their picture of the park with the rabbit's house in it, ask them to consider what the mice might be saying to each other. Ask the children to write the mice's words in the speech bubbles provided in Unit 1 Resource 2: Mouse speech bubbles. Help them to cut out their speech bubbles and stick them onto their picture. (They might want to stick them around the outside and draw a line to the mouse who is speaking in each case.)

Challenge

Children continue the story of what happened to the mice on the snowy day. They write simple sentences.

Homework / Additional activities

Park stories

Ask the children to find and read other stories in the 'Percy the Park Keeper' series, stories set in the snow or about rabbits or mice. If they have any such books at home, they could bring them in to share with the class.

Collins Connect: Unit 1

Ask the children to complete Unit 1 (see Teach → Year 1 → Composition → Unit 1).

Unit 2: Fairy stories

Overview

English curriculum objectives

Reading: Year 1 pupils should be very familiar with key stories, fairy stories and traditional tales, retelling them and considering their particular characteristics.

Writing: Year 1 pupils should be taught to write sentences by:

- saying out loud what they are going to write about
- composing a sentence orally before writing it
- sequencing sentences to form short narratives
- beginning to punctuate sentences using a capital letter and a full stop.

Building towards

Children will explore, discuss and write about a fairy story.

Treasure House resources

- Composition Skills Pupil Book 1, Unit 2, pages 6–7
- Collins Connect Treasure House Composition Year 1 Unit 2
- Photocopiable Unit 2, Resource 1: My pictures for Rumpelstiltskin, page 68
- Photocopiable Unit 2, Resource 2: Speech bubbles for Rumpelstiltskin, page 69

Additional resources

- A retelling of the fairy story Rumpelstiltskin

Introduction

Teaching overview

This unit focuses on the fairy story Rumpelstiltskin. This is one of the many tales included by the German philologists Jakob (1785–1863) and Wilhelm (1786–59) Grimm in their 1812 collection of fairy tales *Children's and Household Tales*, though elements of the tale can be found in far older stories from around the world. Children read a short extract and consider the characters. It provides an opportunity to consider character in fairy stories and to orally rehearse prior to writing.

Introduce the concept

Ask the children what fairy stories they know. Take feedback and ask if they know the story of Rumpelstiltskin. Provide a summary. It would be helpful to have a copy of the full fairy tale to read to the class at some point, perhaps at the close of the session.

Pupil practice

Pupil Book pages 6–7

Get started

Children read the story and add the missing words to the text.

Answers

1. upon	[1 mark]
2. foolish	[1 mark]
3. daughter	[1 mark]
4. wanted	[1 mark]
5. king's	[1 mark]

Try these

Children add their own words to the sentences. Accept appropriate answers.

Possible answers

1. poor/silly

2. greedy

3. normal/ordinary

4. big/grand

5. yellow/dry   [1 mark per acceptable answer]

Now try these

Children draw pictures of the miller and the king at their respective homes. They add speech bubbles showing what each character might be saying. This should be rehearsed beforehand, possibly through role-play or hot-seating. Finally, they write a sentence about the miller telling a lie to the king.

You may wish to use the activities and photocopiables in **Support and Embed** to give differentiated support with these activities.

Support, embed & challenge

Support

Children use Unit 2 Resource 1: My pictures for Rumpelstiltskin to draw the characters and their homes and label each one correctly. Hot-seat the three characters, asking different children to take on each role. Ask the children as the Miller: 'Why did you want to take your daughter to the king?' 'Why did you lie?' 'What will the king do when he learns the truth?' Ask the children as the king: 'Why do you want more gold?' 'Will you be kind to the miller's daughter?' Ask the child as the miller's daughter: 'Do you want to go to the palace?' 'How will you turn straw into gold?' 'Are you scared?' 'Is your father being mean?' After the hot-seating session, ask the children to tell you what the miller and the king in their pictures are saying.

Embed

After the children have drawn their pictures of the miller and the king, ask them to add speech in the speech bubbles provided in Unit 2 Resource 2: Speech bubbles for Rumpelstiltskin. Help the children to cut out their speech bubbles and stick them to their pictures. Ask the children to discuss the miller's lie with a partner. Ask: 'Why did he lie?' 'Will he be found out?' Ask the children to write a sentence about the lie.

Challenge

Children read the full story and write sentences to retell it, starting after the extract.

Homework / Additional activities

Traditional tales to share

Ask the children to find and read other fairy stories or traditional tales at home. They could bring one into school to share with the class or, if they know the story, they could tell it to the class.

Collins Connect: Unit 2

Ask the children to complete Unit 2 (see Teach → Year 1 → Composition → Unit 2).

Unit 3: Fantasy stories (1)

Overview

English curriculum objectives

Reading: Pupils should be very familiar with key stories, fairy stories and traditional tales, retelling them and considering their particular characteristics.

Writing: Pupils should be taught to write sentences by:

- saying out loud what they are going to write about
- composing a sentence orally before writing it
- sequencing sentences to form short narratives
- beginning to punctuate sentences using a capital letter and a full stop.

Building towards

Children will explore, discuss and write about a fantasy story. They will invent another fantastic animal party guest and write a party invitation.

Treasure House resources

- Composition Skills Pupil Book 1, Unit 3, pages 8–9
- Collins Connect Treasure House Composition Year 1 Unit 3
- Photocopiable Unit 3, Resource 1: My fantastic party animal, page 70
- Photocopiable Unit 3, Resource 2: Arthur's party invitation, page 71

Additional resources

- Books involving speaking animals, including Joseph Theobald's *Arthur's Fantastic Party*

Introduction

Teaching overview

This unit focuses on a story about animals who are invited to a party, *Arthur's Fantastic Party* (2005), by Joseph Theobald, a British writer whose books often feature talking animals. Children read a short extract and consider the animals that will be there. It provides an opportunity to consider character in stories and to orally rehearse sentences prior to writing. There are opportunities to write invitations and simple sentences, as well as considering what the guest animals might say as they are invited to the party.

Introduce the concept

Ask the children what stories they know about animals – especially animals who talk! Take feedback and ask: 'Have you ever been to a party?' Ask them to discuss in pairs what happens at a party. 'What games are played?' 'Is there food?' 'Do you have to dress up?' 'Why do people have parties?' Ask the children to talk to each other about any party they have ever been to.

You might like to share the complete story of *Arthur's Fantastic Party* at the end of the session.

Pupil practice

Pupil Book pages 8–9

Get started

Children are asked for labelled drawings of the party's guests. They should have drawn: Arthur, Flora, the three pigs, the wolf and the bears.

[1 mark per acceptable drawing]

Try these

Children add their own words to the sentences. Accept appropriate answers.

Possible answers

1. 'I am excited about my party.'
2. 'It will be fun if lots of animals come to the party.'
3. 'Thanks for inviting us.'
4. 'I love parties.'
5. 'Yes, we'll come to the party too.'

[1 mark per acceptable drawing]

Now try these

Children draw a picture of another fantastic animal who is invited to the party. They draw a speech bubble and add the animal's comments about being invited. They make the invitation and include relevant information such as who the recipient is, and when, where and at what time the party is. They describe the games that Arthur wants to play.

You may wish to use the activities and photocopiables in **Support and Embed** to give differentiated support with the tasks in **Now try these**.

Support, embed & challenge

Support

Focus on **Now try these** question 1 and 2. Children draw their own fantastic animal party guest and write its name in a sentence. They write in a speech bubble what their party guest will say. Unit 3 Resource 1: My fantastic party animal provides the structure for this. Afterwards, ask the children to talk about the party games there might be at Arthur's party.

Embed

Ask the children to focus on **Now try these** questions 3 and 4. For more support, ask the children to complete the invitation on Unit 3 Resource 2: Arthur's party invitation, decorating it appropriately. Ask them to use the space at the bottom of the sheet to describe the party games.

Challenge

Children write sentences about Arthur's fantastic party. They describe what they think might happen when the guests arrive.

Homework / Additional activities

Party fun

Ask the children to interview family members about parties they have been to. If there are photographs that the children are allowed to bring into school, they could share them with the class.

Collins Connect: Unit 3

Ask the children to complete Unit 3 (see Teach → Year 1 → Composition → Unit 3).

Unit 4: Poetry: The senses

Overview

English curriculum objectives

Reading: Year 1 pupils should be taught to develop pleasure in reading, motivation to read, vocabulary and understanding by listening to and discussing a wide range of poems.

Writing: Year 1 pupils should be taught to write sentences by:

- saying out loud what they are going to write about
- composing a sentence orally before writing it
- sequencing sentences to form short narratives
- beginning to punctuate sentences using a capital letter and a full stop.

Building towards

Children will explore and write about the noises they hear at night.

Treasure House resources

- Composition Skills Pupil Book 1, Unit 4, pages 10–11
- Collins Connect Treasure House Composition Year 1 Unit 4
- Photocopiable Unit 4, Resource 1: Night-time sounds, page 72
- Photocopiable Unit 4, Resource 2: What I hear at night, page 73

Additional resources

- Collections of poetry about the senses, especially hearing, and non-fiction texts about hearing, including on-screen texts
- Sound recording of night-time noises, perhaps both in town and countryside

Introduction

Teaching overview

This unit focuses on writing a list of simple sentences based on the senses and inspired by the poem 'Night Sounds' by British children's writer Berlie Doherty (born 1943). The children think of all the sounds they hear at night, label a picture and write a list. There are opportunities to talk about sounds and to practise the sentences orally prior to writing.

This unit can be taught in conjunction with the Key Stage 1 Science curriculum, especially with regard to the many kinds and sources of sound.

Introduce the concept

Ask the children to close their eyes, and then play a sound recording of night-time noise, perhaps in both the town and the countryside. Ask the children to listen very carefully, and afterwards record on a flip-chart what noises they think they heard.

Ask the children what sounds or noises they hear at night, either in the home or outside, especially when they are lying in bed. Discuss the different human-made and natural sounds that can be heard throughout the night.

Find out if the children know the meaning of the word 'nocturnal'. Take feedback and see if they can name any nocturnal animals. Explain that they will read a poem which is about night sounds.

Pupil practice

Get started

After reading the poem, the children write sounds that they believe the objects and animals listed make at night. Accept appropriate answers.

Possible answers

1. twit-ta-woo/hoot

2. tick-tock

3. screech/growl

4. squeak/eek

5. squeak   [1 mark per acceptable answer]

Try these

Children use their own ideas to finish the sentences. Accept appropriate answers.

Possible answers

1. bed

2. owls hooting

3. books on the shelf

4. soap from my bath

5. the soft duvet against my skin
          [1 mark per acceptable answer]

Now try these

Children draw and label a garden at night and a town at night, including as many things as they can that make noises at night. They write a list of the things they can hear at night as they lie in bed, then write a sentence about this. It would be helpful to rehearse this orally first through class discussion.

You may wish to use the activities and photocopiables in **Support and Embed** to give differentiated support with the tasks in **Now try these**.

Support, embed & challenge

Support

Ask the children to focus on **Now try these** question 1 and 2. Unit 4 Resource 1: Night-time sounds provides a template to support the children. Support them as they write their labels. Ask them to share their pictures with a partner, telling them about the details they have drawn.

Embed

Once the children have completed their labeled pictures for **Now try these** questions 1 and 2, ask them to use the structure given in Unit 4 Resource 2: What I hear at night to write a list of sounds, draw a picture and write a couple of sentences about what they can hear as they lie in bed at night.

Challenge

Children write a list poem called 'At night I hear…'. They could also as an extension write a list poem called 'In my school I hear…'

Homework / Additional activities

Night-time noises

Ask the children to listen to all the noises in their home one evening and make a list to share with the class.

Collins Connect: Unit 4

Ask the children to complete Unit 4 (see Teach → Year 1 → Composition → Unit 4).

Unit 5: Poetry: Patterns

Overview

English curriculum objectives

Reading: Year 1 pupils should be taught to develop pleasure in reading, motivation to read, vocabulary and understanding by listening to and discussing a wide range of poems.

Writing: Year 1 pupils should be taught to write sentences by:

- saying out loud what they are going to write about
- composing a sentence orally before writing it
- sequencing sentences to form short narratives
- beginning to punctuate sentences using a capital letter and a full stop.

Building towards

Children will explore, discuss and write about the feelings expressed in a poem.

Treasure House resources

- Composition Skills Pupil Book 1, Unit 5, pages 12–13
- Collins Connect Treasure House Composition Year 1 Unit 5
- Photocopiable Unit 5, Resource 1: Mum and boy's speech bubbles, page 74
- Photocopiable Unit 5, Resource 2: I still love you!, page 75

Additional resources

- Collections of poetry about family and friends, for children to read and browse
- A sample family tree (to help with the homework activity)

Introduction

Teaching overview

This unit focuses on writing simple sentences based on the poem 'Some Things Don't Make Any Sense At All' by the US children's writer Judith Vorst (born 1931). The class reads the poem together and discusses its meaning, especially the feelings of the little boy in the poem. The children will consider a conversation between the boy and his mother and write sentences about their relationship.

There are opportunities to talk about families and people who care for each other, as well as developing the children's sentence writing. There are clear links with the Key Stage 1 PSHE curriculum.

Introduce the concept

Ask the children to talk about their families. Ask: 'How many are in your family? Do you have any brothers or sisters?' Find out if there are any babies in any of the children's families. Ask: 'Do you have any younger brothers or sisters?'

Explain that they will read poem about a little boy who is confused about why his mum has had another baby. They will find out why he feels this way and put his feelings into sentences.

Pupil practice

Get started

After reading the poem, children consider what their families say about them in different situations. They write their own ideas. Accept appropriate answers.

Possible answers

1. I'm a cheeky monkey.

2. I'm a sweetie.

3. I'm a rumble-tum.

4. I'm a sleepy bunny.

5. I'm a grouch.   [1 mark per acceptable answer]

Try these

Children use their own ideas to finish the sentences. Accept appropriate answers.

Possible answers

1. a good boy/girl

2. a funny boy/girl

3. a superstar

4. fun to play with

5. wonderful   [1 mark per acceptable answer]

Now try these

Children draw the boy with his mum and add what they are saying to each other in the speech bubbles. This may need oral rehearsal prior to writing and could involve role-play. Next they draw someone they care about and add speech bubbles. Then they write a sentence to the boy in the poem from his mum telling him that he is still loved, even with the arrival of the new baby.

You may wish to use the activities and photocopiables in **Support and Embed** to give differentiated support with these activities.

Support, embed & challenge

Support

Ask the children to focus on **Now try these** questions 1, 2 and 3. Unit 5 Resource 1: Mum and boy's speech bubbles, provides a template for the children to use for questions 1 and 2. Next, ask the children to draw a picture of themselves with someone they love. Ask them to share their picture with a partner, telling them what the characters are saying to each other.

Embed

After the children have completed their pictures, ask children in the class to share any experience they have had of their mother having another baby.

Sensitively ask them how they felt/feel about the baby and whether they were jealous. If possible, reassure them that it is quite normal to feel jealous by sharing an anecdote of something dreadful you said when a younger sibling was born. Ask the children to fill in the speech bubbles on Unit 5 Resource 2: I still love you! which provides a template for question 5.

Challenge

Children write a short information text called 'My Family'. In this they write information about who is in their family, their pets and any other details, such as family history, the family home, their parents' jobs, and so on.

Homework / Additional activities

My family tree

Ask the children to produce a simple family tree showing their grandparents, parents and their brothers and sisters (you may need to show them what a family tree looks like). They should bring this to school to share with the class.

Collins Connect: Unit 5

Ask the children to complete Unit 5 (see Teach → Year 1 → Composition → Unit 5).

Unit 6: Poetry: My favourite

Overview

English curriculum objectives

Reading: Year 1 pupils should be taught to develop pleasure in reading, motivation to read, vocabulary and understanding by listening to and discussing a wide range of poems.

Writing: Year 1 pupils should be taught to write sentences by:

- saying out loud what they are going to write about
- composing a sentence orally before writing it
- sequencing sentences to form short narratives
- beginning to punctuate sentences using a capital letter and a full stop.

Building towards

Children will explore, discuss and write about a creature living under, on or near the sea.

Treasure House resources

- Composition Skills Pupil Book 1, Unit 6, pages 14–15
- Collins Connect Treasure House Composition Year 1 Unit 6
- Photocopiable Unit 6, Resource 1: My underwater picture, page 76
- Photocopiable Unit 6, Resource 2: All at sea, page 77
- Photocopiable Unit 6, Resource 3: Sea creature, page 78

Additional resources

- Collections of poetry about the sea and the seaside, for children to browse and read
- Non-fiction books and online sites about sea life, for children to browse and read
- Short film/TV clips about sea creatures, such as starfish, dolphins, jellyfish and turtles

Introduction

Teaching overview

This unit focuses on writing simple information sentences and lists based on the poem 'Things I Like in the Sea That Go By Swimmingly' by the Guyanese poet Grace Nichols (born 1950). The class reads the poem together and discusses the structure of the poem: it is written as a list. The children consider creatures that live in or near the sea and describe them in simple words and sentences.

This unit of work lends itself to a cross-curricular theme on 'Under the Sea', or similar.

Introduce the concept

Use pictures and/or a short film clip to give the children an understanding of the sea and/or seaside environment and the creatures that live there. Discuss with the children what they have been looking at.

Ask the children to talk about whether they have ever been to the seaside or to an aquarium (you may need to explain what an aquarium is). Discuss with the class the types of animals you might see on a beach, for example in rock pools, or out at sea.

As the poem is read and discussed, some of the vocabulary (the names of sea creatures) may need further explanation.

Pupil practice

Pupil Book pages 14–15

Get started

After reading the poem, ask the children to find things beginning with specific letters of the alphabet.

Answers

1. crabs [1 mark]

2. octopuses, otters [1 mark]

3. weevers, walruses, whales [1 mark]

4. starfish, seals, sea lions, shrimps [1 mark]

Try these

Children write sentences to describe the sea creatures. Accept appropriate answers.

Possible answers

1. A starfish has lots of pointy arms like a star.

2. A dolphin is grey and friendly.

3. A jellyfish is soft and squishy.

4. A turtle has a patterned shell on its back.

[1 mark per acceptable answer]

Now try these

The children draw a picture to illustrate the poem and use the animal names in the poem to label their picture. Children write a list of other things that can be found in the sea, for example: boats, shipwrecks, caves, rocks, seaweed, coral and sand. They draw an underwater scene adding in six creatures from the poem. They write into speech bubbles what these creatures are saying to each other.

You may wish to use the activities and photocopiables in **Support and Embed** to give differentiated support with the tasks in **Now try these**.

Support, embed & challenge

Support

Ask the children to focus on questions 2 and 3 from **Now try these**. Provide them with Unit 6 Resource 1: My underwater picture and ask them to draw a picture to illustrate the poem, using words from the poem as labels. If appropriate, discuss question 1 with the children. Draw up a group list of further sea creatures and objects. Look together at images of coral reefs and shipwrecks. Discuss characters and settings in films set in the sea or underwater which the children have enjoyed.

Embed

Ask the children to use Unit 6 Resource 2: All at sea to make a list of other things that can be found at sea

for **Now try these** question 1. The resource sheet also provides space for the children to draw a picture of one of their items and write a caption for it.

Challenge

Challenge the children to research information about a sea creature of their choosing. Provide them with Unit 6 Resource 3: Sea creature and ask them to draw a picture and two facts about their chosen animal. Children write their own list poem called 'My Favourite'. They list their favourite foods and keep the same structure as in the poem 'Things I Like In The Sea That Go By Swimmingly'.

Homework / Additional activities

Sea creatures

Ask the children to research information about one of the creatures mentioned in the poem and to write sentences about it. They should bring their work to school to share with the class.

Collins Connect: Unit 6

Ask the children to complete Unit 6 (see Teach → Year 1 → Composition → Unit 6).

Unit 7: Writing instructions (1)

Overview

English curriculum objectives

Reading: Year 1 pupils should develop pleasure in reading, motivation to read, vocabulary and understanding by listening to and discussing a wide range of poems, stories and non-fiction.

Writing: Year 1 pupils should be taught to write sentences by:

- saying out loud what they are going to write about
- composing a sentence orally before writing it
- sequencing sentences
- beginning to punctuate sentences using a capital letter and a full stop.

Building towards

Children will write their own set of instructions using sequencing and command verbs.

Treasure House resources

- Composition Skills Pupil Book 1, Unit 7, pages 16–17

- Collins Connect Treasure House Composition Year 2, Unit 7
- Photocopiable Unit 7, Resource 1: My instructions for growing a beanstalk, page 78
- Photocopiable Unit 7, Resource 2: Welcome to our class, page 79

Additional resources

- A short time-lapse film clip of a bean growing
- Non-fiction texts about growing in general and growing plants, including beans
- A variety of non-fiction texts which include instructions (for example, art and craft books)
- bread, butter, blunt knives
- camera and printer
- materials for making bead bracelets and paper aeroplanes

Introduction

Teaching overview

This unit focuses on a non-fiction instructional text about growing beans and links could be made with the Key Stage 1 science curriculum (growing plants). It provides the opportunity to read instructions and to discuss the features of instruction writing, including the use of command (imperative) verbs and sequences. It also gives children the opportunity to rehearse sentences prior to writing.

Introduce the concept

Ask the children if they have ever grown anything at school or at home. Take feedback and show them a short time-lapse film clip of a bean growing. Ask them to talk to their partners about what happened to the seed and what it needed to grow. Move on to look at some non-fiction books that include instructions and ask the children if they know what an instruction is. Ask whether they follow any instructions at home or at school.

Explain that the children are going to read an extract from a set of instructions about growing a beanstalk (you or they might mention the traditional tale of 'Jack and the Beanstalk' at this time). Use the text to discuss the two main features of instructional text:

1. the use of sequencing (instructions are in the order you need to do them!)
2. the use of command (imperative or 'bossy') verbs, highlighting examples ('Get..', 'Put...', and so on).

You might like to follow up this lesson by asking the children to use a set of instructions to plant beans, sunflowers or some other fast-growing plants.

Pupil practice

Pupil Book pages 16–17

Get started

Children read the information and decide if the items are needed in order to grow a beanstalk.

Answers

1. Yes   [1 mark]

2. No   [1 mark]

3. Yes   [1 mark]

4. No   [1 mark]

5. Yes   [1 mark]

Try these

Children add the missing 'bossy' (imperative) verbs from the text to the sentences.

Answers

1. Get   [1 mark]

2. Put   [1 mark]

3. Place   [1 mark]

4. Add   [1 mark]

5. Pat   [1 mark]

Now try these

Children write instructions for watering the seed and then move on to writing instructions for a playground game and then for buttering bread. They consider what instructions would help a child new to their class know what to do in the mornings (later you might like to get the class to share their ideas and produce a poster based on this activity). In all the sentences, expect the children to use capital letters and full stops. When writing instructions, they should use an imperative verb.

You may wish to use the activities and photocopiables in **Support and Embed** to give differentiated support with the activities in **Now try these**.

Support, embed & challenge

Support

Use Unit 7 Resource 1: My instructions for growing a beanstalk to help children understand the step-by-step nature of instructions. Ask them to use the instructions in the Pupil Book extract to draw the stages of the flowchart, then write the last instruction to water the seed. Next, ask them to carry out question 2 in pairs, drawing the picture together and writing instruction labels. Building up their skills, photograph the children as they butter a slice of bread (question 3) and provide them with the photographs to order. Support them as they write the accompanying instructions (scribing if needed), ensuring they start each instruction with a command.

Embed

Ask the children to carry out **Now try these** question 3, using the extract as a model. Provide them with Unit 7 Resource 2: Welcome to our school, which provides a template for question 4. Remind the children that order is very important here and that they should use command words.

Challenge

Ask the children to write a set of instructions for making a bead bracelet or a paper airplane. Help them source the materials then give their instructions to another child to follow.

Homework / Additional activities

Instructions for making a meal

Ask the children to draw a flowchart depicting the instructional steps for making a meal of their own choice. They can ask their parents for help with this.

Collins Connect: Unit 7

Ask the children to complete Unit 7 (see Teach → Year 1 → Composition → Unit 7).

Review unit 1

A. Stories with familiar settings

This task provides the children with the opportunity to apply and demonstrate the skills they have learned.

Explain to the children that this task provides an opportunity to show their skills independently. Read it through with them and make sure that they have understood what to do.

In A you are looking for evidence of the children's developing understanding of and writing of a story. Significant features to look out for will include:

- use of a familiar setting and characters
- the past tense
- correctly demarcated sentences
- noun phrases
- the conjunction 'and' to link sentences.

B. Instructions

This task provides the children with the opportunity to apply and demonstrate the skills they have learned.

Explain to them that this task provides an opportunity to show their skills independently. Read it through with them and make sure that they have understood what to do.

In B you are looking for evidence of the children's developing understanding of writing instructional text. Significant features to look out for will include:

- imperative (command) verbs
- sequential language
- logical order of instructions
- possible use of diagrams
- a possible statement of purpose at the beginning and a statement at the end
- numbered instructions.

C. Fantasy stories

This task provides the children with the opportunity to apply and demonstrate the skills they have learned.

Explain to them that this task provides an opportunity to show their skills independently. Read it through with them and make sure that they have understood what to do.

In C you are looking for evidence of the children's developing understanding of and writing of a story. Significant features to look out for will include:

- use of a fantasy setting and characters
- the past tense
- correctly demarcated sentences
- noun phrases
- the conjunction 'and' to link sentences.

Unit 8: Writing simple reports (1)

Overview

English curriculum objectives

Reading: Year 2 pupils should develop pleasure in reading, motivation to read, vocabulary and understanding by listening to and discussing a wide range of poems, stories and non-fiction.

Writing: Year 2 pupils should be taught to write sentences by:

- saying out loud what they are going to write about
- composing a sentence orally before writing it
- sequencing sentences
- beginning to punctuate sentences using a capital letter and a full stop.

Building towards

Children will write a report about a bird.

Treasure House resources

- Composition Skills Pupil Book 1, Unit 8, pages 20–21
- Collins Connect Treasure House Composition Year 1, Unit 8
- Photocopiable Unit 8, Resource 1: My picture of a robin, page 80
- Photocopiable Unit 8, Resource 2: My report on a bird, page 81

Additional resources

- A variety of information texts about birds, including simple identification guides
- A clip of a male robin singing
- Websites with child-friendly information about birds, such as the UK's Royal Society for the Protection of Birds

Introduction

Teaching overview

This unit focuses on non-fiction information texts. It provides the opportunity to become familiar with a simple non-fiction report and reading statements of fact. It also gives the children a chance to talk about their chosen bird, rehearsing the sentences prior to writing. This unit has cross-curricular links with science.

It may be that, for your children, the robin is an exotic bird (that is, not native or their country), so you may need to adapt this unit as appropriate.

Introduce the concept

Discuss with children what they know about birds that live in their locality. Ask: 'Can you name any birds?' 'Are there any birds commonly seen in the school grounds?' 'Have you ever seen a robin?' Some children may associate a robin with winter and may have seen them in their gardens. You might like to show a clip of a robin singing.

Explain that they are going to read an extract from a simple non-fiction report about robins. Ask: 'What kinds of information do you expect to hear in such a report?' Take feedback (appearance, habitat, food, and so on) and read the extract.

Pupil practice

Pupil Book page 20–21

Get started

Children read the information and add the missing words to the text.

Answers

1. red		[1 mark]
2. fatter		[1 mark]
3. warm		[1 mark]
4. lovely		[1 mark]
5. fierce		[1 mark]

Try these

Children read the sentences and add their own words. Accept appropriate answers.

Possible answers

1. feathery

2. thin

3. small/sharp

4. wiggly

5. beady   [1 mark per acceptable answer]

Now try these

Children and draw and label a picture, and research information about a robin. They move on to write a sentence about another kind of bird and then one more about birds in winter.

You may wish to use the activities and photocopiables in **Support and Embed** to give differentiated support with the tasks in **Now try these**.

Support, embed & challenge

Support

Use **Now try these** questions 1 and 2 to support the children to write a simple report about robins. Provide them with Unit 8 Resource 1: My picture of a robin, and ask them to draw a robin and label it. Help them to find a fact about robins from the extract to write at the bottom of the page, or support them as they find out their own new fact to use, using information books or the internet. They are reminded to write in full sentences. Talk about another bird that they can name (for example, a penguin) and support them as they verbally create a sentence about this bird and attempt to write it on their whiteboard.

Embed

Ask the children to focus on creating a simple report about a new bird and about birds in winter. Provide books about birds for the children to use for their research. Unit 8 Resource 2: My report on a bird provides a template for the children's writing and illustration.

Challenge

Children research facts about a bird of prey of their choice. They design a fact file and add information and illustrations.

Homework / Additional activities

Bird watching

Ask the children to spend a quarter of an hour looking out of their window or in their neighbourhoods and counting the number of birds they see. They may be able to photograph them. They will tell the class what they saw – how many and, if possible, what types of birds.

Collins Connect: Unit 8

Ask the children to complete Unit 8 (see Teach → Year 1 → Composition → Unit 8).

Unit 9: Writing simple recounts

Overview

English curriculum objectives

Reading: Year 1 pupils should develop understanding by listening to and discussing a wide range of poems, stories and non-fiction.

Writing: Year 1 pupils should be taught to write sentences by:

- saying out loud what they are going to write about
- composing a sentence orally before writing it
- sequencing sentences to form short narratives
- beginning to punctuate sentences using a capital letter and a full stop.

Building towards

Children will write recounts in the first ('I') or third ('he'/'she') persons.

Treasure House resources

- Composition Skills Pupil Book 1, Unit 9, pages 22–23
- Collins Connect Treasure House Composition Year 1, Unit 9
- Photocopiable Unit 9, Resource 1: What I did on my birthday, page 82
- Photocopiable Unit 9, Resource 2: What my friend did yesterday, page 83

Additional resources

- Time-lapse clip of a chick emerging from an egg
- A collection of first-person recount texts – non-fiction and fiction – for children to read and browse

Introduction

Teaching overview

This unit focuses on writing a simple recount based on a text extract about a chick hatching from an egg. The children listen to the extract before reading it independently and then consider how to write in this way – a first-person recount text. The difference between first and third person may need some explanation as children begin to write.

Introduce the concept

Ask: 'Has anyone ever seen a baby hen or chicken – a chick?' 'Do you know what a chick looks like and how it hatches out of an egg?' If possible, show children some time-lapse footage of a chick emerging from an egg. Show photographs of this also.

Read the extract with the children and explain to children that, in the extract, it is the chick himself who is talking (using the first person, or 'I') and not a narrator (who would use third person, or 'he', 'she', 'it' or 'they'). Tell that that this difference in 'point of view' is important when writing: when they are asked to write about their friend at the very end of the unit, will they use 'I' or 'he'/'she'?

Pupil practice

Pupil Book page 22–23

Get started

Children read the sentences and add the missing words to the text. Accept appropriate answers.

Possible answers

1. scratched

2. flapped

3. scrabbled

4. pecked

5. rested   [1 mark per acceptable answer]

Try these

Children write one thing they did at specific times. Accept appropriate answers in the past tense and using the first person.

Possible answers

1. I brushed my teeth.

2. I watched TV.

3. I played football.

4. I went to the beach.

5. I crawled everywhere.

[1 mark per acceptable answer]

Now try these

Children draw the chick in the story, after it has emerged from the shell and started to peck around the farmyard, and themselves as a baby. They think about their last birthday and draw themselves celebrating it. They think about, orally rehearse and then write a sentence about something their friend did the day before. Allow time for the children to discuss this prior to writing.

You may wish to use the activities and photocopiables in **Support and Embed** to give differentiated support with the tasks in **Now try these**.

Support, embed & challenge

Support

After the children have completed **Now try these** questions 1 and 2, use Unit 9 Resource 1: What I did on my birthday to support them as they carry out question 3. Once they have drawn their picture in the box, ask them to tell a partner about their birthday and write a simple sentence about it.

Embed

Ask the children to focus on question 4. Have pairs of children tell each other about something they did yesterday. Ask them to swap partners then tell their new partner what their old partner did yesterday, speaking in complete sentences.

Children use the writing frame (Unit 9 Resource 2: What my friend did yesterday) to write down sentences about what their (original) partner did the day before. They are reminded to check for full stops and capital letters.

Challenge

Ask the children to draw a simple timeline from their birth to the present. They add specific events, for example, starting school. Once it is complete, they write a simple autobiography in sentences in the past tense and using the first person.

Homework / Additional activities

Recounting a visit

Ask children to write a simple recount about a visit they have made. This could be a holiday, a visit to a family member or a school visit. They should use the past tense and first person.

Collins Connect: Unit 9

Ask the children to complete Unit 9 (see Teach → Year 1 → Composition → Unit 9).

Unit 10: Traditional tales

Overview

English curriculum objectives

Reading: Year 1 pupils should be very familiar with key stories, fairy stories and traditional tales, retelling them and considering their particular characteristics.

Writing: Year 1 pupils should be taught to write sentences by:

- saying out loud what they are going to write about
- composing a sentence orally before writing it
- sequencing sentences to form short narratives
- beginning to punctuate sentences using a capital letter and a full stop.

Building towards

Children will explore, discuss and write the ending of a traditional tale.

Treasure House resources

- Composition Skills Pupil Book 1, Unit 10, pages 24–26
- Photocopiable Unit 10, Resource 1: My picture of what happens next, page 84
- Photocopiable Unit 10, Resource 2: What happens next?, page 85

Additional resources

- Copy of the traditional tale 'The Princess and the Pea'
- sticky notes

Introduction

Teaching overview

This unit focuses on a traditional tale, 'The Prince and the Parsnip', and, in particular, the end of the story and what might happen next to the characters. It provides opportunities for prediction, discussion and oral rehearsal, prior to writing.

'The Prince and the Parsnip' is a humorous reworking of 'The Princess and the Pea' (1835) by the Danish author Hans Christian Andersen (1805–75), though his story appears to be based on an older traditional tale.

Introduce the concept

Ask the children what stories they know about princes and princesses. Ask: 'What traditional tales with a prince and a princess do you already know?' 'What do you think a fairy-tale prince and princess would look like?' 'What often happens to them at the end of tales?' Ask the children to share any stories they already know with a partner.

If they do not know the story of 'The Princess and the Pea', it would be useful to read or retell it prior to starting this unit.

Pupil practice

Pupil Book pages 24–26

Get started

Children read the story and add the missing words to the text.

Answers

1. Prince	[1 mark]
2. kind and caring	[1 mark]
3. letters	[1 mark]
4. parsnips	[1 mark]
5. beds	[1 mark]
6. pillow	[1 mark]
7. eight	[1 mark]

Try these

Children read the sentences and decide if they give the correct information as in the story.

Answers

1. True	[1 mark]
2. False	[1 mark]
3. False	[1 mark]
2. False	[1 mark]
5. True	[1 mark]

Now try these

Children begin to write simple sentences using their predictions about what might happen next. They should prepare these orally first. Prior to writing the content of the speech bubbles, the whole class could discuss what the King and Queen could be saying. They could role-play this.

You may wish to use the activities and photocopiables in **Support and Embed** to give differentiated support with the tasks in **Now try these**.

Support, embed & challenge

Support

Reread the extract and ask 'What happens next?' (Remind them of the picture on Pupil Book page 26.) Carry out the tasks in **Now try these** as a group, supporting the children as they write on their individual whiteboards. Role-play a conversation between the King and the Queen. Ask: 'Are they happy about the wedding?' 'Do they think Princess Sue chose well?' Ask the children to write speech bubbles on sticky notes then place them on the illustration in the Pupil Book.

Embed

Ask the children to reread the story then turn to a partner and say what they think happened next. They can ask: 'Did Princess Sue marry Prince Tom or not?' Provide the children with Unit 10 Resource 2: What happens next? and ask them to complete the sheet using their ideas. Explain that if they think that Sue and Tom get married, they should draw that and describe the wedding. However, allow them the freedom to choose a different ending.

Challenge

Ask the children to use Unit 10 Resource 2: Once upon a time to draw a story map for a well-known traditional tale. Ask them to draw a picture of what happens next and write a paragraph to describe the events. They might like to change the ending of the tale they are telling, for example, they could write a different ending to 'Red Riding Hood' where the wolf escapes.

Homework / Additional activities

What happens next?

Ask the children to talk about the endings of stories read at home and make up some different endings to these stories. Where possible, the children could retell and record their new endings ready for telling to the class at school.

Unit 11: Writing simple reports (2)

Overview

English curriculum objectives

Reading: Year 1 pupils should develop pleasure in reading, motivation to read, vocabulary and understanding by listening to and discussing a wide range of poems, stories and non-fiction.

Writing: Year 1 pupils should be taught to write sentences by:

- saying out loud what they are going to write about
- composing a sentence orally before writing it
- sequencing sentences
- beginning to punctuate sentences using a capital letter and a full stop.

Building towards

Children will write a simple recount text about an animal.

Treasure House resources

- Composition Skills Pupil Book 1, Unit 11, pages 27–28
- Photocopiable Unit 11, Resource 1: Fantastic zebras and giraffes, page 86
- Photocopiable Unit 11, Resource 2: My animal report, page 87

Additional resources

- A variety of information texts and links for websites about birds and animals
- A short clip of a helper bird

Introduction

Teaching overview

This unit focuses on non-fiction information text and continues work begun in Unit 8. It provides the opportunity to become increasingly familiar with non-fiction text and reading statements of fact. It also provides an opportunity for children to talk about their chosen animal, rehearsing the sentences prior to writing. This unit has links with the science curriculum.

Note that, for your children, the helper bird may not be an 'exotic' species, so be prepared to swap or adapt Units 8 and 11 as appropriate.

Introduce the concept

Remind the children of the information text about robins they read in Unit 8. Tell them that they are now going to read more information about another bird, though this one lives farther away in a different country.

Ask the children whether they know of any birds that do not live in their home country. As a class, research birds that live in other countries or that migrate to different countries. Show the children a short clip about the helper bird and spend a few minutes discussing with them what they have seen. Talk about the habitat and the kinds of animals that live there.

Explain to the children that they will read an extract from a text about the helper bird. Invite them to listen to the text about the helper bird prior to reading it independently.

Pupil practice

Pupil Book pages 27–28

Get started

Children read the information and add the missing words to the text.

Answers

1. Africa [1 mark]
2. big animals [1 mark]
3. ticks, skin [1 mark]
4. eats [1 mark]
5. good food [1 mark]
6. zebras and buffaloes [1 mark]
7. lion [1 mark]
8. helper [1 mark]

Try these

Children read the sentences and decide if they give the correct information. They decide if the sentences are true or false.

Answers

1. false [1 mark]
2. true [1 mark]
3. true [1 mark]
4. false [1 mark]
5. true [1 mark]

Now try these

Children research information about zebras or giraffes, choosing at least three facts to compose full sentences about. They draw a picture of their animal and label it.

You may wish to use the activities and photocopiables in **Support and Embed** to give differentiated support with the tasks in **Now try these**.

Support, embed & challenge

Support

Provide the children with Unit 11 Resource 1: Fantastic zebras and giraffes, which provides the children with a selection of facts to use in their report. Provide them with Unit 11 Resource 2: My animal report and ask them to choose three facts about their preferred animal and write these to create the report. They draw a labeled illustration.

Embed

Provide the children with a selection of suitable information books and ask them to find three facts about their chosen animal. Ask them use Unit 11 Resource 2: My animal report to write their report, writing their facts as full sentences and drawing an illustration.

Challenge

Children research a bird of their choice and design a fact file. They add information and illustrations.

Homework / Additional activities

Animal investigations

Discuss any recent visits to zoos, farms or the countryside where animals have been seen. Ask the children to research information on one of the animals and create a fact file. If they have not made any recent visits, ask them to write a fact file about an animal that they hope to see one day.

Unit 12: Stories in familiar settings (2)

Overview

English curriculum objectives

Reading: Year 1 pupils should be very familiar with key stories, fairy stories and traditional tales, retelling them and considering their particular characteristics.

Writing: Year 1 pupils should be taught to write sentences by:

- saying out loud what they are going to write about
- composing a sentence orally before writing it
- sequencing sentences to form short narratives
- beginning to punctuate sentences using a capital letter and a full stop.

Building towards

Children will write a story about a naughty pet.

Treasure House resources

- Composition Skills Pupil Book 1, Unit 12, pages 29–31
- Photocopiable Unit 12, Resource 1: How naughty!, page 88
- Photocopiable Unit 12, Resource 2: What a naughty animal, page 89

Additional resources

- A variety of stories set in familiar settings for children to browse and read

Introduction

Teaching overview

This unit focuses on stories in familiar settings and continues work begun in Unit 1. It provides the opportunity for children to become increasingly familiar with such texts, discussing setting, plot and character. It also gives them the chance to rehearse their ideas and sentences orally prior to writing.

The base text is an extract from *Sam the Big, Bad Cat*, written by Sheila Bird.

Introduce the concept

Ask: 'Does anyone have pets at home?' If they do, find out which pets they have. If any of the children have cats, ask them to talk about the cats and their habits. Ask: 'Do you know what a vet is?' 'Have any of you ever been to a vet?' 'What was it like?' Discuss the fact that few animals like going to the vet.

Ask for predictions once they know that they are going to read an extract from a story called *Sam, the Big, Bad Cat*. Ask: 'What do you think the cat might do?' 'How might it behave badly?'

Pupil practice

Pupil Book pages 29–31

Get started

Children read the extract and add the missing words to the text.

Answers

1. Sam		[1 mark]
2. the vet		[1 mark]
3. his bed		[1 mark]
4. the table		[1 mark]
5. to bed		[1 mark]

Try these

Children read the sentences and decide which give the correct information.

Answers

1. true		[1 mark]
2. false		[1 mark]
3. false		[1 mark]
4. true		[1 mark]
5. true		[1 mark]

Now try these

The children think of a scene in which an animal is naughty. They draw their scene and write sentences to go with their picture.

You may wish to use the activities and photocopiables in **Support and Embed** to give differentiated support with the tasks in **Now try these**.

Support, embed & challenge

Support

Support these children with ideas for their story: a puppy has run away with a sock, or stolen the dinner off the table, a cat has torn up a child's homework, or is looking as if he's about to eat the budgie, a monkey at the zoo has stolen someone's phone or a seagull at the beach has swooped down and stolen a pie. Give the children the top half of Unit 12 Resource 1: How naughty! (one box and one set of lines) and ask them to draw a picture and write one sentence about the naughty thing the animal did.

Embed

Ask the children to discuss ideas for a naughty animal story with a partner. Ask them to imagine two scenes – first, the naughty act, then what happens next. Ask them to use Unit 12 Resource 1: How naughty! to capture their two-part story.

Challenge

Ask the children to plan and write a more complete story using Unit 12 Resource 2: What a naughty animal.

Homework / Additional activities

Naughty pets!

Are there any stories of real naughty pets in children's families? If so, ask children to write a few sentences about their stories. They might like to retell the stories in the classroom as well.

If not, ask the children to question members of their families about what animal they would like to keep as a pet. Ask them to write a sentence about what pet each member of the family would like.

Unit 13: Fables (1)

Overview

English curriculum objectives

Reading: Year 1 pupils should be very familiar with key stories, fairy stories and traditional tales, retelling them and considering their particular characteristics.

Writing: Year 1 pupils should be taught to write sentences by:

- saying out loud what they are going to write about
- composing a sentence orally before writing it
- sequencing sentences to form short narratives
- beginning to punctuate sentences using a capital letter and a full stop.

Building towards

Children will recount a well-known fable.

Treasure House resources

- Composition Skills Pupil Book 1, Unit 13, pages 32–33
- Photocopiable Unit 13, Resource 1: My ending, page 90
- Photocopiable Unit 13, Resource 2: The Lion and the Mouse, page 91

Additional resources

- *Aesop's Fables* and books with modern retellings

Introduction

Teaching overview

This unit focuses on writing a simple recount based on the fable 'The Lion and the Mouse'. The children listen to the story and retell it in their own words. You will need to explain to them that a fable has a moral: it teaches the reader something about how to behave.

'The Lion and the Mouse' is one of best-known fables told by the ancient Greek writer Aesop, who lived in the 6th century BCE. He wrote his fables for adults but later they came to be seen as stories with moral messages for children.

Introduce the concept

Ask: 'Do you know any stories about lions or mice?' Take feedback from the children and explain that they will read an extract from a story about what happens between a lion and mouse when they meet. Ask for predictions about what might happen.

At this point it may be appropriate to tell children that a fable is a special type of story that carries a message. 'The Lion and the Mouse' is a fable. At the end of the unit, read the whole story to the class. Discuss the end of the story. Was this what the children expected? If it was different to their own ending ask: 'Do you prefer Aesop's ending or your own?' At the end of the story, it would be good to discuss with the children what they think the message is: the usual interpretation is that we all depend on one another, however powerful we are.

Pupil practice

Pupil Book pages 32–33

Get started

Children read the story and add the missing words to the text.

Answers

1. sleeping	[1 mark]
2. playing	[1 mark]
3. mouse	[1 mark]
4. mouse	[1 mark]
5. a net	[1 mark]
6. free	[1 mark]

Try these

Children read the sentences and decide if they give the correct information as in the story.

Answers

1. false	[1 mark]
2. false	[1 mark]
3. true	[1 mark]
4. false	[1 mark]
5. true	[1 mark]

Now try these

Children recount the fable orally to their partners deciding on their own ending, then writing their version of the story, illustrating the ending. They use the illustrations in the text to support them.

You may wish to use the activities and photocopiables in **Support and Embed** to give differentiated support with the tasks in **Now try these**.

Support, embed & challenge

Support

Children use the story map in the Pupil Book to retell the fable orally. Using Unit 13 Resource 1: My ending they draw a picture of the ending and write a sentence underneath.

Embed

Children use the story map as a prompt for the oral retelling of the tale creating their own ending. They then use Unit 13 Resource 2: The Lion and the Mouse to write their version of the fable. They should be reminded to check for capital letters and full stops and that they have used the past tense.

Challenge

Children learn another Aesop fable to tell, for example, 'The tortoise and the hare' or 'The fox and the stork'.

Homework / Additional activities

Aesop's Fables

Ask the children to find one or two more *Aesop's Fables* and to read one of them. They could share one of the tales with the class.

Unit 14: Writing instructions (2)

Overview

English curriculum objectives

Reading: Pupils should develop pleasure in reading, motivation to read, vocabulary and understanding by listening to and discussing a wide range of poems, stories and non-fiction.

Writing: Pupils should be taught to write sentences by:

- saying out loud what they are going to write about
- composing a sentence orally before writing it
- sequencing sentences
- beginning to punctuate sentences using a capital letter and a full stop.

Building towards

Children will write a sequenced instruction text about keeping worms.

Treasure House resources

- Composition Skills Pupil Book 1, Unit 14, pages 34–35
- Photocopiable Unit 14, Resource 1: My flowchart for keeping a worm, page 92
- Photocopiable Unit 14, Resource 2: How to keep a worm, page 93

Additional resources

- Jars of earth with earthworms and/or video clips of earthworms
- A variety of books, brochures and leaflets featuring instructions for children to browse and read

Introduction

Teaching overview

This unit focuses on non-fiction instruction text and continues work begun in Unit 7. It provides another opportunity to practise the writing of this type of text and for children to talk about the text, rehearsing the sentences prior to writing. Links could be made with the science curriculum.

Introduce the concept

If possible, have on display bottles of earth with earthworms and/or show clips of earthworms.

Discuss with children what they know about worms. Ask: 'Have you seen any in the school garden? At home? What do you think worms do? How do they survive? What do you think you need to do if you want to keep worms as pets?'

Remind them of previous work on instructions and the main features of instruction text (use of sequencing and command verbs).

Pupil practice

Pupil Book page 34–35

Get started

Children read the information and decide if the items are needed in order to keep a worm as a pet.

Answers

1. Yes   [1 mark]

2. No   [1 mark]

3. Yes   [1 mark]

4. Yes   [1 mark]

5. No   [1 mark]

Try these

Children decide if the sentences are commands.

Answers

1. Command   [1 mark]

2. Command   [1 mark]

3. Not a command   [1 mark]

4. Command.   [1 mark]

5. Not a command.   [1 mark]

Now try these

Children use the flowchart to rehearse orally how to keep a worm as a pet. They write a set of instructions for this, using the adverbials to begin the command sentences. They continue to practise instruction writing by drawing a flowchart showing how to make a sandwich. They then add the instructions.

In children's answers look for chronologically ordered (sequenced) commands and the use of adverbials to begin the sentences.

You may wish to use the activities and photocopiables in **Support and Embed** to give differentiated support with the tasks in **Now try these**.

Support, embed & challenge

Support

Support the children as they use the flowchart in the Pupil Book to orally explain how to catch and keep a pet worm. When they are confident with the stages, ask them to use Unit 14 Resource 1: My flowchart for keeping a worm as a template for their own flowchart showing the steps for keeping a worm as a pet.

Embed

After orally rehearsing the process using the flowchart in the Pupil Book, ask the children to write a set of instructions using the structure provided on Unit 14 Resource 2: How to keep a worm and the opening prompts. They add drawings to show what to do. Next, ask the children to draw a flowchart showing the process for making a sandwich (with their own filling). Ask those who are more confident to write command sentences for each point.

Challenge

Children draw they own flowchart depicting the instructional steps for a task of their own choosing.

Homework / Additional activities

Instructions at home

Ask the children to consider what instructions are used every day at home. This might be instructions for making a meal (recipes), putting together an item of flat-pack furniture or playing a game. Children should make a list and be ready to share it in class.

Review unit 2

A. Writing non-fiction reports

This task provides the children with the opportunity to apply and demonstrate the skills they have learned.

Explain to the children that this task provides an opportunity to show their skills independently. Read it through with them and make sure that they have understood what to do.

In A you are looking for evidence of the children's developing understanding of and writing of reports. Significant features to look out for include:

- the use of sub-headings to structure the information into sections
- the present tense
- correctly punctuated sentences
- the use of pictures or illustrations.

B. Recount

This task provides the children with the opportunity to apply and demonstrate the skills they have learned.

Explain to the children that this task provides an opportunity to show their skills independently. Read it through with them and make sure that they have understood what to do.

In B you are looking for evidence of the children's developing understanding of and writing of recounts. Significant features to look out for include:

- correctly punctuated sentences
- the past tense
- the use of the conjunction 'and' to join sentences
- the events of the day in sequential order.

C. Writing stories

This task provides the children with the opportunity to apply and demonstrate the skills they have learned.

Explain to the children that this task provides an opportunity to show their skills independently. Read it through with them and make sure that they have understood what to do.

In C you are looking for evidence of the children's developing understanding of and writing of narrative. Significant features to look out for will include:

- the past tense
- the use of time language to structure events – long, long ago, then, later
- correctly demarcated sentences
- the conjunction 'and' linking sentences
- a beginning, middle and end to the story.

Unit 15: Writing simple reports (3)

Overview

English curriculum objectives

Reading: Pupils should develop understanding by listening to and discussing a wide range of poems, stories and non-fiction.

Writing: Pupils should be taught to write sentences by:

- saying out loud what they are going to write about
- composing a sentence orally before writing it
- sequencing sentences
- beginning to punctuate sentences using a capital letter and a full stop.

Building towards

Children will research and write a report about polar bears.

Treasure House resources

- Composition Skills Pupil Book 1, Unit 15, pages 38–40
- Photocopiable Unit 15, Resource 1: My polar bear report, page 94
- Photocopiable Unit 15, Resource 2: Polar bear fact file, page 95

Additional resources

- A terrarium with stick insects or images of stick insects
- A variety of information texts about animals and their habitats for children to browse and read

Introduction

Teaching overview

This unit focuses on non-fiction information reports and continues work begun in Unit 8. It provides a further opportunity for children to become familiar with non-fiction reports and reading and writing statements of fact, and to rehearse their sentences prior to writing. The unit makes cross-curricular links with the science curriculum.

Introduce the concept

If possible, show the children a terrarium or similar container with stick insects, or pictures of one. Can the children spot the insects?

Ask the class if they know the meaning of the word 'camouflage'. Take predictions and then look up the meaning of the word in a dictionary. Ask: 'Can you think of anything else in nature which uses camouflage?' Discuss children's ideas about why animals might use camouflage. Explain that they are going to read an extract from a book which gives examples of animals that use camouflage for different reasons.

Pupil practice

Pupil Book page 38–40

Get started

Children read the information and add the missing words.

Answers

1. camouflage	[1 mark]
2. where they hide	[1 mark]
3. hunt	[1 mark]
4. hide	[1 mark]
5. leaves	[1 mark]

Try these

Children read the sentences and decide if they give the correct information.

Answers

1. true	[1 mark]
2. true	[1 mark]
3. true	[1 mark]
4. false	[1 mark]
5. true	[1 mark]

Now try these

Children research information about polar bears, choosing at least three facts to compose sentences about. They draw a labelled picture and write their three facts as a report.

You may wish to use the activities and photocopiables in **Support and Embed** to give differentiated support with the tasks in **Now try these**.

Support, embed & challenge

Support

Support these children as they research their facts about the polar bear. Help them to make useful notes from books and the internet. Children use Unit 15 Resource 1: My report on the polar bear to draw a polar bear. They use the writing frame to support them as they add facts beneath it one at a time. Remind them to write in sentences.

Embed

Children research facts about polar bears and, using Unit 15 Resource 2: Polar bear fact file, create a fact file. This resource sheet encourages the children to combine their facts into a paragraph of text and provides a space for them to add an illustration. They are reminded to write in full sentences.

Challenge

Children research another creature that uses camouflage and write facts about it. They add labelled diagrams to their writing. They check they have correctly punctuated their sentences.

Homework / Additional activities

Polar animals

Ask the children to research facts about other animals that live in polar regions. They could write a short list of facts and bring them into school to share. They may draw pictures or bring in photographs or books. If they know a website that has useful information about animals in polar regions, they could share this, too.

Unit 16: Fables (2)

Overview

English curriculum objectives

Reading: Year 1 pupils should be very familiar with key stories, fairy stories and traditional tales, retelling them and considering their particular characteristics.

Writing: Year 1 pupils should be taught to write sentences by:

- saying out loud what they are going to write about
- composing a sentence orally before writing it
- sequencing sentences to form short narratives
- beginning to punctuate sentences using a capital letter and a full stop.

Building towards

Children will write a recount of a fable and predict and write an ending.

Treasure House resources

- Composition Skills Pupil Book 1, Unit 16, pages 41–42
- Photocopiable Unit 16, Resource 1: My ending for the fable, page 96
- Photocopiable Unit 16, Resource 2: My recount of the fable, page 97

Additional resources

- *Aesop's Fables* and books with modern retellings or new fables

Introduction

Teaching overview

This unit focuses on writing a simple recount based on the fable 'Meg, Mum and the Donkey'. It continues work on fables begun in Unit 13 and provides additional practice at writing recount sentences. The children listen to the story, discuss it and retell it in their own words.

This modern retelling by Simon Puttock is based on Aesop's 'The Man, His Son and the Donkey'. The moral is not to take on the advice of others, but to make up your own mind.

Introduce the concept

Ask the children if they remember a previous unit called 'The Lion and the Mouse' and remind them of the kind of tale known as a fable. Take their feedback and explain that they will read an extract from another fable. This one is called 'Meg, Mum and the Donkey'.

Remind the children that a fable has a message. Ask them to talk to each other about the message in the story of the lion and the mouse. Tell the children that the fable they will read today has a message. Ask them to think about what it might be, as they read. You might like to discuss this at the end of the lesson. Read the story together.

Pupil practice

Pupil Book page 41–42

Get started

Children answer the questions orally with a partner.

Answers

1. They are going to the market. [1 mark]
2. The girl is riding and mum is walking. [1 mark]
3. The donkey feels tired because they are heavy. [1 mark]
4. They were tired because they carried the donkey. [1 mark]

Try these

Children read the sentences and write them in the correct sequence.

Answers

1. Meg and Mum took their donkey to market. [1 mark]
2. Mum said, "Up you go!" [1 mark]
3. Mum rode. [1 mark]
4. Mum and Meg both rode. [1 mark]
5. Mum and Meg carried the donkey. [1 mark]
6. Mum and Meg needed a rest. [1 mark]
7. The donkey got away! [1 mark]

Now try these

First ask children to recount the tale orally to their partners using the story map. Then they predict what Mum and Meg will do next, draw their predictions and write the accompanying sentences.

You may wish to use the activities and photocopiables in **Support and Embed** to give differentiated support with the tasks in **Now try these**.

Support, embed & challenge

Support

Help the children as they practise using the story map on Pupil Book page 42 to retell the story in their own words. Ask them to discuss different endings with a partner, prompt them with ideas if need be: 'Do they catch the donkey but treat it better? Do they buy a car or bicycles? Do they buy another donkey? Do they just walk home?' Children use Unit 16 Resource 1: My ending for the fable to support their prediction for Mum and Meg. Once they have drawn an illustration and written an accompanying sentence, ask them to retell the story adding their predicted ending.

Embed

Children use the story map in the Pupil Book as a prompt for the oral retelling of the tale. After practising the story and making it their own, ask them to use Unit 16 Resource 2: My recount of the fable to write a recount of the tale. Remind them to check for capital letters and full stops and that they have used the past tense. Tell them to decide on an ending for the story and to draw it on the resource sheet, writing a final sentence at the bottom.

Challenge

Children read another fable from *Aesop's Fables*. They retell it in their own words and share this with the class.

Homework / Additional activities

All about Aesop

Ask the children to find out about Aesop – who he was and when he wrote the fables (see Unit 13). Children could write a short fact file about him.

Unit 17: Stories in familiar settings (3)

Overview

English curriculum objectives

Reading: Year 1 pupils should be very familiar with key stories, fairy stories and traditional tales, retelling them and considering their particular characteristics.

Writing: Year 1 pupils should be taught to write sentences by:

- saying out loud what they are going to write about
- composing a sentence orally before writing it
- sequencing sentences to form short narratives
- beginning to punctuate sentences using a capital letter and a full stop.

Building towards

Children will write a recount of a story about a frog's day.

Treasure House resources

- Composition Skills Pupil Book 1, Unit 17, pages 43–44
- Photocopiable Unit 17, Resource 1: The frog's day, page 98
- Photocopiable Unit 17, Resource 2: My recount of 'Doing Nothing!', page 99

Additional resources

- A collection of non-fiction texts about frogs as well as any stories about frogs for children to browse and read
- Other books by Petr Horácek, such as *Animal Opposites* and *Silly Suzy Goose*

Introduction

Teaching overview

This unit focuses on stories in familiar settings and continues work in Units 1 and 12. It provides a further opportunity for the children to become familiar with such texts, discussing setting, plot and character. It also gives them the chance to rehearse their ideas and sentences orally prior to writing. There may be links to the science curriculum. This unit would be especially enjoyable for children if it could be combined with a visit to a school wildlife pond.

Petr Horácek (born 1974), the author of the story extract used in this unit, is a well-known Czech-born children's writer and illustrator, now living in the UK. Children might like to read more of his animal books.

Introduce the concept

Discuss with the children the story of *Sam the Big, Bad Cat* and ask them to retell the story. Point out that it is set in a place that they know well (a home) and that many stories are set in such places. Make children aware that the extract they will read in this unit is also set in a familiar but different place – a pond – and is about a creature they know something about. Ask them to list the facts they know about frogs.

Pupil practice

Pupil Book pages 43–44

Get started

Children read the extract and add the missing words to the text.

Answers

1. pond   [1 mark]

2. rock   [1 mark]

3. nothing   [1 mark]

4. sat   [1 mark]

5. hopped, climbed, jumped   [1 mark]

Try these

Children read the sentences and decide if they give the correct information.

Answers

1. false   [1 mark]

2. true   [1 mark]

3. false   [1 mark]

4. true   [1 mark]

5. false   [1 mark]

Now try these

Children use the story map to help them orally retell and then write the full story of the frog's day. Make sure that they understand why the frog has to hop away from each predator.

You may wish to use the activities and photocopiables in **Support and Embed** to give differentiated support with these activities.

Support, embed & challenge

Support

Work in a group with children who need support to tell a shortened version of the story with just two predators (for example, the snake and the bird). Place sticky notes over the other animals on the storyboard in the book. Practise telling the story together, saying a sentence each. When the children are confident, ask the children to use Unit 17 Resource 1: The frog's day to draw two captioned pictures about the story.

Embed

Ask the children to practise telling the story with a partner, using the story map on Pupil Book page 44. Children use the structured plan in Unit 17 Resource 2: My recount of 'Doing Nothing!' to support their retelling of the frog's day. Remind them to use the past tense.

Challenge

Children write about their own day. They draw a story map and write sentences to accompany this.

Homework / Additional activities

Map of a day

Ask the children to interview members of their family about their day. They choose one person and draw a story map based on that person's day.

Unit 18: Writing simple reports (4)

Overview

English curriculum objectives

Reading: Year 1 pupils should develop understanding by listening to and discussing a wide range of poems, stories and non-fiction.

Writing: Year 1 pupils should be taught to write sentences by:

- saying out loud what they are going to write about
- composing a sentence orally before writing it
- sequencing sentences
- beginning to punctuate sentences using a capital letter and a full stop.

Building towards

Children will write a simple report about their home.

Treasure House resources

- Composition Skills Pupil Book 1, Unit 18, pages 45–46
- Photocopiable Unit 18, Resource 1: My home, page 100
- Photocopiable Unit 18, Resource 2: Information report on my home, page 101

Additional resources

- A variety of information texts about houses and homes across the world
- Websites or short film clips to support the content

Introduction

Teaching overview

This unit focuses on non-fiction information reports and continues work begun in Units 8 and 11 and continued in Unit 15. It provides children with a further opportunity to become familiar with non-fiction reports and reading and writing statements of fact. It also gives them the opportunity to rehearse their sentences orally prior to writing and to check that their statement sentences are punctuated correctly.

The unit will link well with Key Stage 1 Geography (houses around the world).

Introduce the concept

Ask the class to draw a picture of their home – the place where they live. They should then share their drawing with their partner and discuss similarities and differences. Ask them what they know about the types of houses in which people live in different countries. Ask: 'Do any of you know anyone who lives in another country in a different type of house?'

Take feedback and then explain that the extract is about the different homes people live in across the world. Before reading the text, ask for predictions as to the different types of houses that exist.

Pupil practice

Pupil Book pages 45–46

Get started

Children read the information and add the missing words.

Answers

1. homes		[1 mark]
2. high up		[1 mark]
3. noisy		[1 mark]
4. quiet		[1 mark]
5. water		[1 mark]
6. wheels		[1 mark]

Try these

Children read the sentences and decide if they give the correct information. They tick the true sentences.

Answers

1. false	[1 mark]
2. true	[1 mark]
3. false	[1 mark]
4. false	[1 mark]
5. true	[1 mark]

Now try these

Children discuss the different houses and move on to draw the inside of their homes, labelling the rooms. They write statement sentences about their homes and, if they have them, gardens.

You may wish to use the activities and photocopiables in **Support and Embed** to give differentiated support with these activities.

Support, embed & challenge

Support

Support the children as they discuss the homes in the photographs (in the Pupil Book) and their own home. Using Unit 18 Resource 1: My home, children draw the inside of their homes and, with support, add three statement sentences about their homes. The resource sheet provides structure and supports the children as they write one sentence at a time.

Embed

Children write statement sentences about their homes and add a labelled picture of their house, showing the different rooms and the garden (if they have one), adding additional labels for important items such as their bed. Unit 18 Resource 2: Information report on my home supports this writing, and encourages the children to write a short paragraph of text.

Challenge

Ask the children to write sentences about other homes they know – perhaps the home of a relative or friend. They should add sentences about how it is different from their own home.

Homework / Additional activities

Home plan

Ask the children to draw and label a plan of their home showing the different spaces. You might like to show them a simple example. They can ask for help at home to do this. These plans can be shared in class as part of a discussion about different homes.

Unit 19: Information writing

Overview

English curriculum objectives

Reading: Year 1 pupils should be taught to develop pleasure in reading, motivation to read, vocabulary and understanding by listening to and discussing a wide range of poems.

Writing: Year 1 pupils should be taught to write sentences by:

- saying out loud what they are going to write about
- composing a sentence orally before writing it
- sequencing sentences to form short narratives
- beginning to punctuate sentences using a capital letter and a full stop.

Building towards

Children will write an information text about their own school day.

Treasure House resources

- Composition Skills Pupil Book 1, Unit 19, pages 47–49
- Photocopiable Unit 19, Resource 1: My 'school day' flowchart, page 102
- Photocopiable Unit 19, Resource 2: My 'school day' storyboard, page 103

Additional resources

- Collections of poetry on the theme of school
- A teaching clock
- *Twiddling Your Thumbs* by Wendy Cope
- *The River Girl* by Wendy Cope

Introduction

Teaching overview

This unit focuses on writing simple information sentences based on a poem about school life and provides additional practice on writing non-fiction sentences. The children listen to and discuss the poem, and then use the theme to write a simple account of their school day. The unit could be related to telling the time as well as to the PSHE curriculum, by encouraging children to share their thoughts and feelings about school.

The poem 'Time for School' is by the celebrated British poet Wendy Cope (born 1945). She has written two excellent collections of poetry for children *Twiddling Your Thumbs* (1989) and *The River Girl* (1991). You might like to have these available for children to browse and explore.

Introduce the concept

Ask the children to talk about their school day. Ask: 'Which parts of the day do you like the most? Why? Do you remember your first day at school? How did you feel?'

Explain to children that they are going to read a poem about a day at school from the point of view of a young child. Read the poem with the children and discuss what is happening at different parts of the day. Discuss whether the same things happen at their school.

You may find it useful to have a teaching clock available when discussing the various activities of the school day and reading the poem.

Pupil practice

Get started

Children read the poem and write five things the children do at school during the day.

Possible answers

Any five of the following:

1. Read books.

2. Do sums.

3. Write stories.

4. Paint pictures.

5. Run around, laugh and shout – play outside.

6. Sing, clap, stamp their feet.

7. Have lunch.   [1 mark per acceptable answer]

Try these

Children read the sentences and write them in the correct sequence.

Answers

1. Hello teacher. Bye-bye Mum.   [1 mark]

2. Books to read and sums to do.   [1 mark]

3. When the bell rings, we go out, Run around and laugh and shout.   [1 mark]

4. Then at last, it's time to eat.   [1 mark]

5. More play, more work, all afternoon.   [1 mark]

6. Half past three. Home time has come.   [1 mark]

Now try these

Children draw pictures to represent the different parts of their school day. They add the time of each activity and then write simple sentences describing what happens at these times and in the activities.

You may wish to use the activities and photocopiables in **Support and Embed** to give differentiated support with these activities.

Support, embed & challenge

Support

Ask the children to choose which day they are going to write about – perhaps a day when they do PE. Ask them to discuss the day with a partner, choosing four events to cover in their information text. Unit 19 Resource 1: My 'school day' flowchart provides a flowchart template to support the children, as they draw their pictures and add a phrase to each as a label.

Embed

Ask the children to choose a day of the week to cover in their information text. Ask them to then choose three events from the day to write about. Provide them with Unit 19 Resource 2: My 'school day' storyboard and ask them to draw a picture for each activity and write a sentence. Ask them to write the time for the start of each activity, recapping on time and how it should be written. Display a written version of key times on the board.

Challenge

Ask the children to write sentences about their favourite part of the school day. Explain to them that they must say why it is so.

Homework / Additional activities

My weekend

Ask the children to complete either another flowchart or a storyboard of their weekend to show how it differs from their school days.

Unit 20: Fantasy stories (2)

Overview

English curriculum objectives

Reading: Year 1 pupils should be taught to develop pleasure in reading, motivation to read, vocabulary and understanding by listening to and discussing a wide range of poems.

Writing: Year 1 pupils should be taught to write sentences by:

- saying out loud what they are going to write about
- composing a sentence orally before writing it
- sequencing sentences to form short narratives
- beginning to punctuate sentences using a capital letter and a full stop.

Building towards

Children will plan and write their own story about a journey into space on a rocket.

Treasure House resources

- Composition Skills Pupil Book 1, Unit 20, pages 50–53
- Photocopiable Unit 20, Resource 1: My rocket, page 104
- Photocopiable Unit 20, Resource 2: My rocket: plan and story, page 105

Additional resources

- A variety of stories set in other worlds
- A clip of a rocket launch and similar

Introduction

Teaching overview

This unit provides the opportunity to discuss stories that are not set in familiar places but in other worlds, and continues work begun in Unit 3. It has as its base a poem set in imaginary worlds – building a rocket and travelling in space and to other planets. It also gives an opportunity for children to rehearse their ideas and sentences orally prior to writing.

Introduce the concept

Show a clip of a real rocket launch.

Discuss with the children whether they have read any stories set in space or watched any TV programmes or films set in space or on the Moon. Take feedback.

Ask: 'Have you ever tried to build a rocket?' Discuss their attempts at doing so with building blocks, with recyclable materials, and so on. Ask: 'What design did you follow?'

Explain that they will be reading a poem about a child who wants to build a rocket to take her friends into space.

You might like to end the lesson by showing children footage of the first people to walk on the Moon after the *Apollo 11* landing on 29 July 1969. This will set the scene for the homework activity.

Pupil practice

Pupil Book pages 50–53

Get started

Children read the poem and answer the questions.

Answers

1. On a trip to the Sun. [1 mark]
2. It is too hot. [1 mark]
3. It has no air. [1 mark]
4. The child has not thought about how it will land. [1 mark]
5. The child finds it harder than she thought to build a rocket. [1 mark]

Try these

Children read the sentences and decide if they give the correct information. They tick the true sentences.

1. false [1 mark]
2. false [1 mark]
3. true [1 mark]
4. true [1 mark]
5. false [1 mark]

Now try these

Children design and draw a rocket they would like to travel in. They label it and write a simple story about their journey into space. They should plan it and orally rehearse it before writing. Drawing a simple story map would be helpful as they plan their story.

You may wish to use the activities and photocopiables in **Support and Embed** to give differentiated support with the tasks in **Now try these**.

Support, embed & challenge

Support

Look at images of rockets and discuss possible adventures the children could have in their rocket. Support the children with story ideas: They travel to a planet with funny aliens, they whizz around the Earth but they get travel-sick and go home, they go to the moon and wave at the Earth, they land on a star and meet an angel, and so on. Children draw and label their rocket in the space provided on Unit 20 Resource 1: My rocket. They write a sentence about their journey under their labelled diagram.

Embed

Children use a story map to plan their story and then write the story in the space provided on Unit 20,

Resource 2: My rocket: plan and story. They are reminded what their story map should include and to check for correct sentence punctuation. The resource sheet is on two pages: the first provides space for the story plan and text; the second provides space for them to draw and label their rocket. Encourage the children to use interesting vocabulary to describe their rocket.

Challenge

Children reread the poem and continue the story. Does the child build a rocket and where does she go with his friends? What do they discover on their journey?

Homework / Additional activities

Men on the Moon

Ask the children to find out about the first Moon landing – when did it happen? They should research the names of the astronauts and those who first walked on the Moon, and be prepared to share what they have discovered with the class.

Review unit 3

A. Information writing

This task provides the children with the opportunity to apply and demonstrate the skills they have learned.

Explain to the children that this task provides an opportunity to show their skills independently. Read it through with them and make sure that they have understood what to do.

In A you are looking for evidence of the children's developing understanding of and writing of reports. Significant features to look out for include:

- the use of sub-headings to structure the information into sections
- the present tense
- correctly punctuated sentences
- the use of pictures and/or a map.

B. Instructions

This task provides the children with the opportunity to apply and demonstrate the skills they have learned.

Explain to the children that this task provides an opportunity to show their skills independently. Read it through with them and make sure that they have understood what to do.

In B you are looking for evidence of the children's developing understanding of and writing of instructions. Significant features to look out for will include:

- imperative (command) verbs
- sequential language
- logical order of instructions
- possible use of diagrams
- a possible statement of purpose at the beginning and a statement at the end
- numbered instructions.

C. Traditional tales and fables

This task provides the children with the opportunity to apply and demonstrate the skills they have learned.

Explain to children that this task provides an opportunity to show their skills independently. Read it through with them and make sure that they have understood what to do.

In C you are looking for evidence of children's developing understanding of and writing of traditional tales and fables, especially the ordering of events. Significant features to look out for will include:

- the beginning, middle and end of the story represented in the story map
- clear development of ideas
- events in sequential order
- correct labelling of events in the plot.

My picture of the park

Draw a picture of the park. Then add the rabbit's house. Write some labels for your pictures.

© HarperCollins*Publishers* 2017

Mouse speech bubbles

Write in the speech bubbles what you think the mice are saying.

My pictures for Rumpelstiltskin

Draw the king.

Draw the king's palace.

The king lives in a _____.

Draw the miller.

Draw the miller's house.

The miller lives in a _____.

Speech bubbles for Rumpelstiltskin

Write in the speech bubbles what you think the prince is saying.

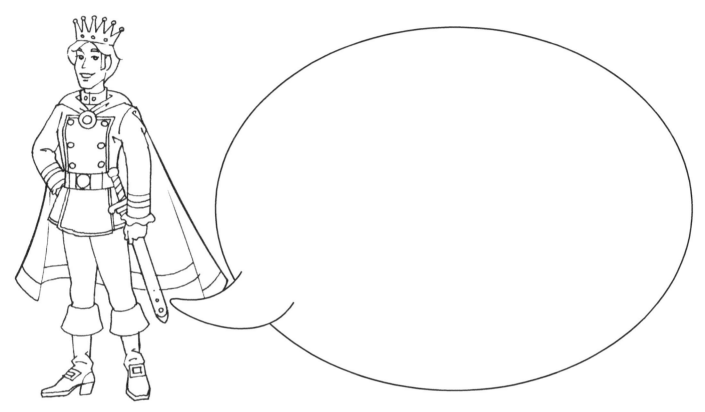

Write in the speech bubbles what you think the miller is saying.

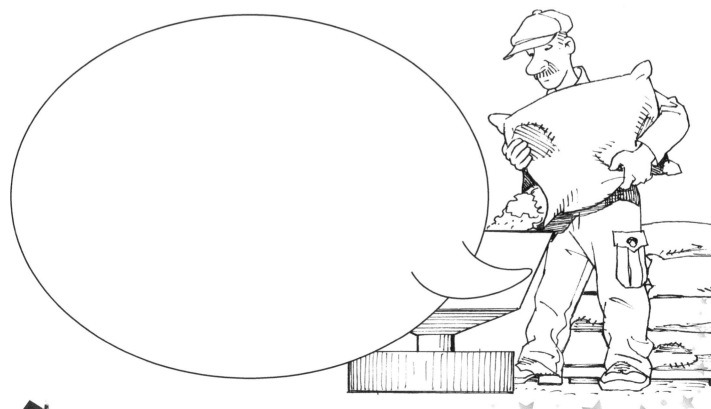

My fantastic party animal

Draw a picture of your fantastic party animal.

My fantastic party animal is called _____.

Write in the speech bubble what your party animal said when they were invited to the party.

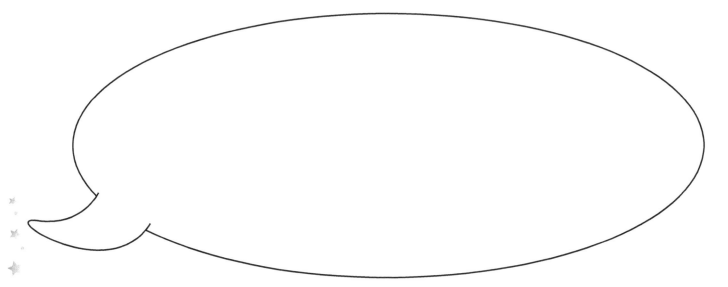

Arthur's party invitation

Finish the party invitation here. You may decorate it.

Name of animal: _____.

Arthur would like to invite you to his Fantastic Animal Party on _____.

It will be held at _____.

Time: _____.

What games will be played at Arthur's party? Write a few sentences about the games that you will play at the party.

_____

_____

_____

_____

_____

_____

Night-time sounds

Draw a picture of night-time outside in a garden.

What sounds can be heard? Label your picture.

Draw a picture of night-time in a town.

What sounds can be heard? Label your picture.

What I hear at night

In my home at night I can hear...

1. _____

2. _____

3. _____

Draw a picture of one of these sounds you can hear.

_____

Write two sentences about noises you can hear outside at night.
Remember to use a capital letter and a full stop.

_____

_____

_____

_____

Mum and boy's speech bubbles

Boy

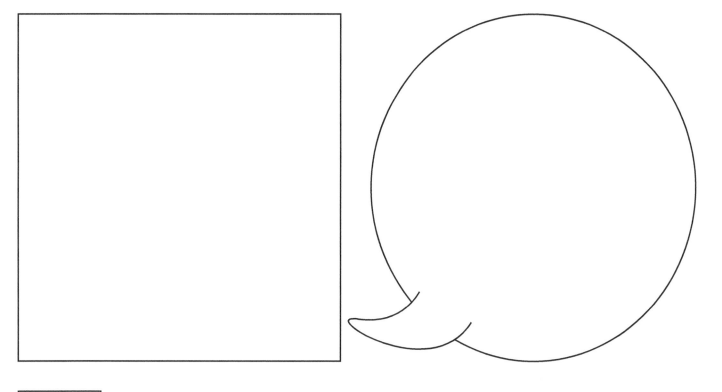

Mum

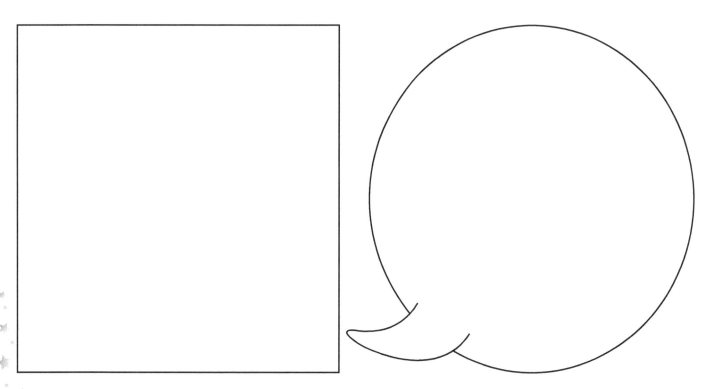

I still love you!

Write in the speech bubble what Mum says to the little boy about how much she loves him.

Write sentences here to the boy from his mum. The sentences tell him that she still loves him just as much, even though she has had a new baby. Start with 'I'.

I _____

_____

_____

_____

_____

_____

My underwater picture

Draw an underwater picture and add creatures from the poem. Label the creatures with their correct names.

All at sea

Make a list of other things that can be found in the sea.

1. _____

2. _____

3. _____

4. _____

5. _____

6. _____

Choose a sea creature and write three facts about it.

Sea creature: _____

1. _____

2. _____

3. _____

Sea creature

Draw a picture of a sea creature.

Write three facts about your sea creature.

1. _____

2. _____

3. _____

My instructions for growing a beanstalk

Draw a flowchart to show what you need to do to grow a beanstalk. The first part has been done for you.

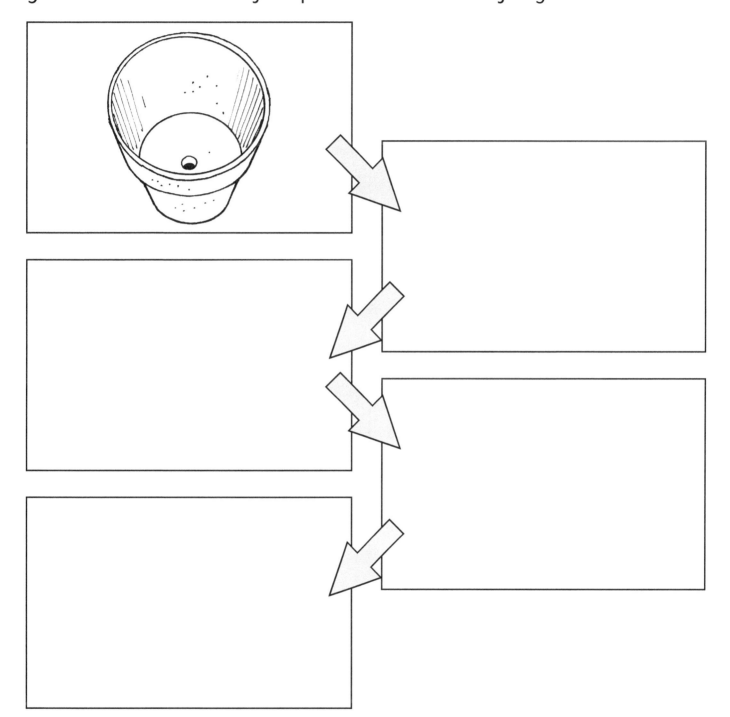

Write an instruction to tell people to water the seed.

_____

_____

Welcome to our class

Write instructions below to help a new child know
what to do in your class at the beginning of the day.

	Draw a picture here to show what to do.
First _____ _____ _____	
Next _____ _____ _____	
Then _____ _____ _____	
After that _____ _____ _____	
Finally _____ _____ _____	

My picture of a robin

Draw a picture of a robin. Label its beak, wings, feathers and red breast.

Write one fact about a robin here. Write it in a full sentence with a capital letter and a full stop.

_____

_____

My report on a bird

Write a full sentence or two about your bird.

_____

_____

_____

_____

_____

Draw your bird and label it.

Write a fact about birds in winter. Use a full sentence.

_____

_____

_____

What I did on my birthday

Draw a picture of you on your birthday.

Write the next sentence of the story.

_____

Write three more sentences to finish the story.

_____

_____

_____

What my friend did yesterday

Draw a picture of your friend and what he or she did yesterday.

Write sentences about what your friend did yesterday.

You will need to ask them first!

_____

_____

_____

_____

_____

Check your sentences for full stops and capital letters.

© HarperCollins*Publishers* 2017

My picture of what happens next

Draw what happens next in the story in the space below.

Write the next sentence of the story.

_____

Write three more sentences to finish the story.

_____

_____

_____

Once upon a time

Draw a story map of a traditional tale.

Draw another picture to show what might happen after the story has finished.

Write three sentences about your picture, telling the reader what happened next.

_____

_____

_____

_____

_____

Fantastic zebras and giraffes

Read these facts. Choose three to use in your report.

Zebras

Every zebra has a different pattern of stripes.

A zebra can run as fast as a car.

A zebra can sleep standing up.

Every year millions of zebra travel thousands of miles across Africa.

Zebras live in Africa.

Zebras eat grass.

A zebra has black skin under its striped fur.

Giraffes

Giraffes are the tallest land animal.

A giraffe's tongue can be 50 cm long.

A group of giraffes is called a tower.

Giraffes live in Africa.

Giraffes spend all day eating leaves and twigs.

Giraffes only sleep for two hours a day.

My animal report

My animal is a _____ .

Write facts here about your animal. Write in sentences.

_____

_____

_____

_____

_____

Draw a labelled diagram of your chosen animal.

How naughty!

Draw a picture of the animal doing something naughty.

Write two sentences about what is happening in your picture.

Draw a picture to show what happens next.

Write two sentences to go with this picture.

What a naughty animal

What naughty animal will be in your story?

_____

What is the naughty thing the animal does?

_____

What happens at the end of the story?

_____

Writing my story

Write your story here. Check for capital letters and full stops.

_____

_____

_____

_____

Draw the picture to go with your story.

My ending

Use the story map in the Pupil Book to tell your partner the tale.

What happens after the lion gets out of the net? Draw a picture.

Write a sentence to explain what happened in your picture.

_____

_____

The Lion and the Mouse

Retell the fable of 'The Lion and the Mouse', using the story map in the Pupil Book to help you. The first sentence has been written for you.

One day a lion was sleeping in the shade under a tree.

_____

_____

_____

_____

_____

Draw a picture to show what happened at the end of the story.

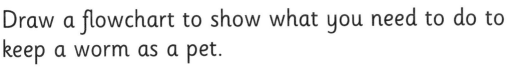

My flowchart for keeping a worm

Draw a flowchart to show what you need to do to keep a worm as a pet.

Number the things you must do.

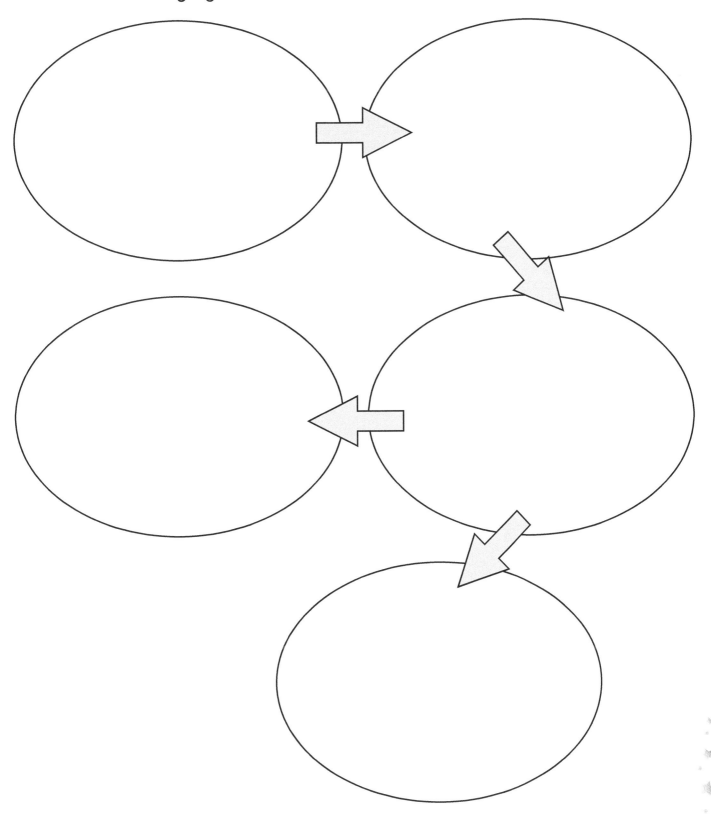

How to keep a worm

Write instructions below for keeping a worm as a pet.

	Draw a picture here to show what to do.
First _____ _____ _____	
Next _____ _____ _____	
Then _____ _____ _____	
After that _____ _____ _____	
Finally _____ _____ _____	

My polar bear report

Draw a picture of a polar bear.

Write one fact about a polar bear here.

_____

_____

Write one fact about a polar bear here.

_____

_____

Write one fact about a polar bear here.

_____

_____

Polar bear fact file

Write facts about polar bears in the space below.
Write in sentences.

_____

_____

_____

_____

_____

_____

_____

Draw a picture of a polar bear.

My ending for the fable

Draw a picture of what happens next to Mum and Meg.

Write a sentence to go with your picture.

_____

_____

My recount of the fable

Recount the fable of 'Meg, Mum and the Donkey'.
The first sentence is done for you.

<u>One day Meg and Mum got ready to go to market.</u>

_____

_____

_____

_____

_____

Draw a picture to show what happened to Mum and Meg after the donkey had run away.

[drawing box]

Write a sentence about what happened to go with your picture.

_____

_____

© HarperCollins*Publishers* 2017

The frog's day

Draw a picture of the frog sitting at the bottom of the pond.

Write a sentence about what is happening in your picture.

Draw pictures to show what happens to the frog.

Write a sentence to go with these pictures.

My recount of 'Doing Nothing!'

The frog has to escape from three creatures who want to catch him. Write the story of the frog's day. The first sentence has been written for you.

One day a frog was sitting at the bottom of a pond.

Draw a picture to go with your story.

My home

Draw a picture of the inside of your home here.

Write one sentence about your home here.

_____

_____

Write one sentence about your home here.

_____

_____

Write one sentence about your home here.

_____

_____

Information report on my home

Write an information report about your home. Write in sentences. Tell the reader all about what your home is like.

_____

_____

_____

_____

Draw a picture of your house. Label the different rooms and some of the important things in the rooms (like your bed!)

My 'school day' flowchart

Draw a flowchart to show the different things you do each day at school.

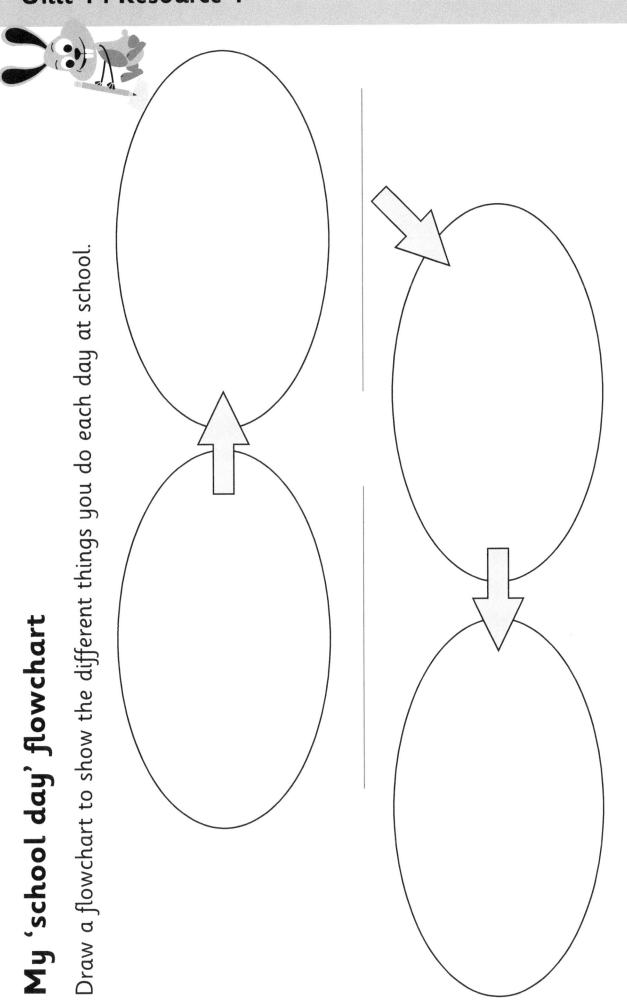

Add a label to each part of the day.

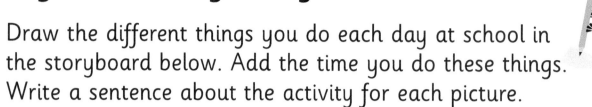

My 'school day' storyboard

Draw the different things you do each day at school in the storyboard below. Add the time you do these things. Write a sentence about the activity for each picture.

What I do at school – pictures	Write a sentence
Time: _____	_____ _____ _____ _____
Time: _____	_____ _____ _____ _____
Time: _____	_____ _____ _____ _____

My rocket

Draw a picture of your rocket. Label the different parts.

Write a sentence about where you want to go in your rocket and who will go with you.

_____

_____

My rocket: plan and story

Draw the story map of your journey to show how it starts, what happens in the middle and how it ends.

Write the story of your journey in the space below. Write in sentences and check that you have used capital letters and full stops.

Draw a picture of your rocket here.